Testimonials

On November 13, 1982, Ron Miller personally leased an L-1011 from Delta Airlines and took 300 Vietnam Veterans to the dedication of the Vietnam Veterans Memorial in Washington, D.C. As a result of his remarkable efforts, President Ronald Reagan asked him to form the Georgia Vietnam Veterans Leadership Program, a volunteer organization that was recognized as one of the best in the nation by President George H.W. Bush, who presented Ron and the GVVLP with his prestigious Thousand Points of Light award for their service to Veterans and their families. Hopefully this story will encourage all Americans to reach out to others with their assistance.

Governor Mike Huckabee

Readers will come away from Ron's book inspired and knowing that one man can make a difference. Ron devoted his life to help Veterans— to help those willing to give all for our country. Read Ron's book and you will have a checklist how to make a difference in your life, your community; your country.

Col. Leo Thorsness, USAF (Ret.), Medal of Honor, Vietnam, was held prisoner in Hanoi, Vietnam, for six years. Author, *Surviving Hell: A POW's Journey*

Ron Miller's book is an amazing story of how a dedicated and disciplined person can go from the son of a farmer in the muddy Delta, to become an Army Officer of more than 20 years service. Ron is a war veteran who continued to serve the American Veterans and family members in achieving their deserved benefits and has worked hard as a political activist to protect those benefits. I salute Ron for all he has done: "Serving those who have served." His book clearly shows that the American Dream is still there for those who want it.

First Sergeant Nicky D. Bacon, USA (Ret.), Medal of Honor, Vietnam Retired Director of the Arkansas Department of Veterans Affairs.

America has no kings or queens, no Dukes or Duchesses, but we do have nobility. America's nobility is called Veterans—Ron Miller is part

of that nobility. His remarkable story is typical of so many veterans who come from humble origins and contribute so much to the country we love—they never stop serving. Men and women like Ron are true patriots who prove their love of America by supporting and defending her, unlike the multitude of faux patriots who claim to love America but do nothing to support and defend her. And men and women like Ron give lie to the media lies of the Vietnam veteran as a homeless helpless miscreant. The Vietnam Veteran is a productive and patriotic citizen as is Ron and his book is a perfect example of one Vietnam veteran's extraordinary service to the country they love.

Maj. Gen. Patrick Brady, USA (Ret.), Medal of Honor, Vietnam
Author, *Dead Men Flying* about Dust-off pilots in Vietnam

Ron Miller is a "Veteran's Veteran." Not only did he serve with distinction in Vietnam, he helped bring his fellow veterans of that war home the right way as a key leader in the Vietnam Veterans Leadership Program (VVLP). After helping to make that program a success, Ron continued to serve veterans and help them get businesses going and their lives (in some instances) back on track. Ron Miller is one of the most unselfish men I know. He understands the meaning of service to one's country and service to his fellow veterans. My old boss, Ronald Reagan, liked to talk about the spirit of America being reflected in that principle of "neighbor helping neighbor." Ron Miller exemplifies that spirit, and his story needs to be read by others who can learn from what he has done to help his fellow veterans.

Tom Pauken, Chairman, Texas Workforce Commission
former Director, ACTION

Ron's book is long overdue. What a story of commitment and dedication that extends through Veteran's issues into his devotion to his community and to our nation. Reading this book is truly uplifting and inspiring! Ron has richly blessed my life through his friendship.

Jo Anne Shirley, Chairman of the Board of Directors for the
National League of American Prisoners and Missing, 1995-2009

Ron Miller is one of God's great gifts to the American Veteran. Many of the war fighters of yesterday's wars as well as today's have benefited tremendously due to Ron's dedicated efforts over the years. This story highlights many of those efforts beginning at the lower echelons of support to the highest within our Nation—all done with perfection.

Lieutenant General Jerry Max Bunyard, U.S. Army (Ret).

Ron, thank you for sharing your autobiography and putting together the plane trip to the dedication of the Vietnam Veterans Memorial 27 years ago. It changed not only your life but all of us 300 participants on your "Great Adventure." You showed us all what one person can do with a dream and an uncompromising spirit.

John Medlin, Producer/Director Documentary, "Memories of War,"
29th Civil Affairs Company, U.S. Army I Corps, Vietnam 1969-70

This is probably the best book of its type to be published so far. It is remarkable, accurate, timely, from the heart and a must read.

Commissioner and General Pete Wheeler,
Georgia Department of Veterans Service

Outstanding job of authorship! This book is not just good...It's outstanding. Wow, what a story you have lived, had to tell, and have told so well. It was a tour-d'pleasure from start to finish.

Rev. Jim Pat Mills, National Chief of Chaplains,
Veterans Chaplain Association, Washington, D.C.

Contents

Dedication 9

Foreword 11

Chapter 1: Vietnam Veteran: Home at Last 17

Chapter 2: President Ronald Reagan 57

Chapter 3: President George H.W. Bush... 61

Chapter 4: Senator Bob Dole.. 69

Chapter 5: General Raymond G. Davis, Medal of Honor, USMC (Ret) 77

Chapter 6: Bob Hope.. 83

Chapter 7: Vice President Dick Cheney.. 95

Chapter 8: General William C. Westmoreland.................................. 99

Chapter 9: Governor Mike Huckabee 107

Chapter 10: Winthrop Paul Rockefeller 113

Chapter 11: Senator John McCain... 117

Chapter 12: Movie: Perfume River.. 121

Chapter 13: POW Documentary—Beyond Courage:
Surviving Vietnam as a POW 125

Chapter 14: National League of Families of American Prisoners and Missing
in Southeast Asia.. 131

Chapter 15: President Bill Clinton 137

Chapter 16: Home Box Office.. 141

Chapter 17: Jeff Foxworthy... 143

Chapter 18: Lee Greenwood.. 145

Chapter 19: Arkansas State University Reserve Officers Training Corps
Hall of Heroes 147

Chapter 20: Vietnam Veterans Memorial, Atlanta, Georgia 149

Chapter 21: A Special Thank You.. 153

About the Author.. 155

Dedication

This book is dedicated to my family
Mr. Albert M. Miller (WWI)
Mrs. Lula Ann Miller
Ecil Miller
Ralph Miller (WWII)
Bill Miller (WWII)
Owen Miller (WWII)
Elaine Miller McCoy
Betty Miller Smith
Bob Miller (Korea)
Marsha Miller Midkiff
and to all Veterans

Foreword

I had originally titled my book, "From the Cottonfields of Arkansas to A Ride in the Limo with The President." After I finished the book it became obvious to me that the title should be changed to "Vietnam Special Flight, Inc." Leasing a L1011 aircraft from Delta Airlines and taking 300 Vietnam veterans to the dedication of the Vietnam Veterans Memorial in Washington, D.C., on November 13, 1982 completely changed my life and took me down a road that I could never imagine.

I was born and raised on a 40-acre cotton farm in Mississippi County, West Ridge, Arkansas. I started picking and chopping cotton at 6 years of age. The cotton industry was dependent upon manual labor, instead of being mechanized the way it is now. There were nine children in my family, six boys and three girls. Working was a sun-up to sun-down job, hot as Hades in the summer and sometimes the work lasted until December.

I remember pulling cotton bowls with some ice on the ground. I was always dreaming of getting away from the farm, my favorite pastime was leaning on my hoe and looking up in the sky to occasionally see an airplane high in the sky with contrails floating behind the plane. I said to myself a million times, "I wish I was a pilot and enjoying the ride!"

Fate was kind to me after I graduated high school. Good friends of my parents were visiting from Chicago, and I talked Mom and Dad into letting me go back with them in order to get a full-time job. My biggest motive was to get off the farm. To my surprise, they agreed and gave me $50.00 and one suitcase, and I was on my way to make it in the big city.

Everywhere I applied for a job, they would ask my age. I was 17 years old. They would say, "You will be drafted!" and they would not hire me. After I ran through the $50.00, I had to work on a hay farm outside of the city to make enough money to ride the bus home. It stopped 18 miles from our home. I hitch hiked home, walked in and asked my parents about going to college.

My brother's wife, Betty, was a school teacher. She, my Mom and I drove over to Arkansas State College, which is now a University. We walked into the Dean of Student's Office to see Dean Moore. I will never forget my Mom's words to Dean Moore, "My son wants to go to college. We don't have enough money to afford all the fees, but this boy will work his way through!" Dean Moore's response was, "If he wants to go bad enough, we will find him a job!" I worked in the WigWam, the student's gathering place for food, drinks and socializing.

During my last year in ROTC, the Army came out with a special flight training course. They had eleven slots. The cadets would take training that led to a private license at the local airport. I took the test and got the last slot, completed the course, which led to the Army Helicopter Pilot and Multi-Engine Flight School. I flew for over twenty years in the United State Army in a career I thoroughly enjoyed, which included three tours as a Helicopter Pilot in Vietnam. So! You see if you dream and wish hard enough, your dreams can come true.

Although my family did not have much money, we always had good food to eat and a nice home, thanks to my parents Albert M. and Lula Ann Miller. We killed hogs for meat, placed some in a smoke house for the winter, chickens for eggs and food, cows for milk and butter.

In addition, my mother, who was a saint to me then and now, worked as the Manager at the school lunch room for years. In addition to the extra money she made at the job, she and her co-workers were allowed to take home the remainder of leftovers to their family. I once said at the supper table, "I am tired of eating the same food at home as I did at school." My father, who was a strong, quiet man who did not lecture us very much, looked directly at me and said, "You better be happy that you have this much!" I never said another word about the food that my family provided to me, then and now.

Author, Ron Miller.

Albert M. Miller
U.S. Army, World War I

Ralph M. Miller
U.S. Army, World War II

Billy R. Miller, Sr.
U.S. Navy, World War II

Owen T. Miller
U.S. Navy, World War II

Bobby R. Miller
U.S. Marines, Korean War

Ronnie M. Miller
U.S. Army, Viet Nam War

Chapter 1

Vietnam Veteran

Home At Last

I served three tours in Vietnam as a helicopter and multi-engine airplane pilot and served 20 years in the U.S. Army. My Mother and Father moved from Alabama to Arkansas in the 1930s, cleared 40 acres of land, and grew cotton for 40 years. They were very patriotic individuals, and they raised nine children with those values. My Father and five boys served in the military; I was the only one who made it a career. One brother was wounded so badly in the Normandy landings that he was written off as dead; he survived.

A brother contracted Tuberculosis as a result of his military service. Even with all the difficulties, I never once heard my parents or my brothers say that they regretted serving their country.

There are many stories within my military career, and I will relate three incidents that occurred prior to my leaving the Army in 1980.

In 1967, I was acting as a helicopter safety consultant to the John Wayne movie, "The Green Berets," being filmed at Fort Benning, Georgia. It was my responsibility to ensure that all helicopter scenes were shot safely. One scene required Tim Hutton to hang underneath a helicopter while stealing stacks of tin out of a Navy yard. I was standing next to Mr. Wayne with a radio and in contact with the chopper. The plan was for a stuntman to get on the load of tin as the chopper lifted off. They were having difficulties with camera angles, so Mr. Wayne turned to me, laid his hand, the size of a catcher's mitt, on my shoulder and said, "This is a very important scene in the movie and I want the chopper to take off with Mr. Hutton underneath." My respect and admiration for Mr. Wayne clouded my safety responsibilities, and I told the pilot to take off. He did, and needless to say, Mr. Hutton had an experience that I'm sure he talked about the rest of his life.

In January 1968, I attended an Aerospace Management course for a semester at USC Los Angeles. We could not wear our uniforms because the University thought that we might create problems with the students. While there, I wrote "The Joey Bishop" T.V. show and asked for four tickets. We received them and on the way to the studio, stopped off at a lounge next door and had a couple of drinks to loosen up a bit. A friend and I wore our uniforms, and we were seated in the front row of the studio. Regis Philbin came out first to warm up the audience. He spotted us in the front row and mentioned that Mr. Bishop had served in the military. Mr. Bishop came out for his monologue and spotted us seated there. He asked me to come on stage and give him a few marching commands. Feeling no pain, I called him to attention, marched him off the stage, then turned to R. Philbin and said the show was ours. Mr. Bishop and the audience loved it. I called everyone I knew in Arkansas and told them to watch the show that night. Needless to say, it was a very big hit in West Ridge, Arkansas. (Population 12 on the weekends!)

In 1970, while stationed at Fort Lewis, Washington, I was pulling weekend duty as the Post Senior Staff Duty Officer. I was at home, and received a call from the Military Police that Jane Fonda and several other individuals were on post trying to talk a group of GIs into disobeying orders from their officers and to talk them out of serving in Vietnam.

When I arrived, she and her friends had been apprehended and taken to the MP office. I told the MP's to put them in a classroom instead of a jail cell. She and the group called us lifers, among a few other things. Ms. Fonda had on a long maxi leather coat that looked as if she had slept in it for quite awhile. She had no makeup on, and her hair was stringy. If I had passed her on the street, I would not have given her a second glance, nor would I have recognized her. They wanted to leave, and at once. I informed them that the only person who could release them was the Provost Marshal, a Colonel, and that I would call him. I did and he was playing tennis and told me to tell them that he would be there after the match. He made it clear to me that I should tell them exactly that. Forty-five minutes later, he arrived in his tennis outfit. Needless to say, Ms. Fonda and her cohorts were furious and that's the reason he did it. He asked them to sign a release; she refused, the Provost Marshal made a note of that and we took them off post and dropped them off on the freeway. We never saw Ms. Fonda again at Fort Lewis.

I was stationed at Fort Benning, Georgia in 1962, flying the Sikorsky H-34, Cargo helicopters when James Meredith attempted to enroll at Ole Miss in Oxford, Mississippi. As the readers will remember, it caused a firestorm that resulted in the President sending in the Military to ensure that he could attend the University. Our unit was alerted to fly to Millington Naval Air Station in Memphis, TN and transport U.S. Marshals to Oxford to provide protection for Mr. Meredith. As I recall, we had six of the huge helicopters, myself and my great friend, Gene Beyer flew one. I met Gene, from Abilene, Texas, on my first day in the Army when we reported to Fort Benning to go through Officers Basic Training. We were both awaiting orders to attend helicopter flight school at Camp Wolters, Texas.

After we finished the officers' course, he talked me into going to Paratrooper school and he wanted me to go to Ranger School. I declined Ranger School because it was too cold at that time of year, and I hated snakes which were plentiful in the swamps in Florida. After Airborne training, we departed for Texas for four and a half months of primary helicopter flight training, then off to Fort Rucker, Alabama for helicopter cargo training for an additional four and a half months. We were then both assigned to Fort Benning and shared a house off post. It was a great time to be in the military; we worked hard and played hard. The Officer clubs were rocking and rolling in those days as there were plenty of good looking women and the music never stopped. To give you an example, Frank Sinatra, Jr. and his band played at the main club for a weekend.

As luck would have it, Gene was at my retirement luncheon at Fort Sam Houston, Texas in San Antonio, another great party town that I almost stayed in. Gene retired as a full Colonel, a superb Officer and a true friend. My school, Arkansas State University played his Alma Mater, Texas A&M in 2008 at College Station. We surprised everyone and won the game. Gene and his wife, Jenny, live on a ranch south of Austin. I stayed with them for a few days. On the way home from the game Gene informed me that I would be sleeping with the goats for the next few days for beating the Aggies.

We took the Marshals to the Oxford airport where they departed for the University campus. We spent the night sleeping in our helicopters and could hear gunfire for most of the evening. Marshals were on duty for 24 hours straight and the MP's were flown into Millington, and we flew them to Oxford to relieve the Marshals. We picked the Marshals up at the airport and transported them to a tent city a few miles from the airport for rest. They were exhausted, one had a broken leg, six had received gunshot wounds and all their clothes were soaked with tear gas. Fumes came up into the cockpit, which caused us to open our windows and fly at an angle to keep the gas out of our eyes.

That was a sad time in the history of our country. The American people finally understood that equal rights meant equal rights for all. My Alma Mater enrolled the first blacks during my time there in the fifties with zero problems. A fellow black ROTC student and friend, Fred Turner, Jr., retired as a Lieutenant Colonel. I met him some time after that when he visited the University and remarked to him that he must have married one good-looking lady, because their daughter had become Miss America. He laughed and said that he had. We did experience one instance of racism; our ROTC unit was being transported to a military base for some training and we stopped in the country for lunch. We were in our ROTC uniforms, entered a restaurant and took our seats with two blacks with us, including Fred, and the staff refused to serve them. They did not make a fuss, left the restaurant, and went to the bus. I went out and asked them if they wanted me to bring them some sandwiches, but they declined. I was upset at their treatment, but they never showed any resentment, which told me a lot about them as a person, one with lots of class.

There is another very interesting fact about the integration of Ole Miss. Major General Edwin Walker, United States Army (Ret.) was in Oxford during this time. He was previously the Commanding General of a Division in Germany and was relieved of his command for his Anti-Communist indoctrination program for the troops, he subsequently resigned. He came to the attention of an individual that would shortly become a household name, Lee Harvey Oswald. Oswald staked out General Walker's home in Dallas and on April 10th, 1963, he attempted to kill the General while he was sitting at a desk in his home. The bullet was deflected by hitting the side of a window frame. On November 22nd, 1963, Lee Harvey Oswald assassinated President John F. Kennedy in Dallas.

During this time period, I was the personal pilot for Major General Frank Mildren, Commanding General of the 3rd Infantry Division at Wurtzberg, Germany. I flew him in a Huey almost every day during the two years that I was his pilot.

On June 25th, 1963, I was notified to pick up the General and take him to Frankfurt, Germany for a very special occasion. I was not told until we departed that the General and other Division Commanders would be meeting with President Kennedy. We landed a few miles from the airport and took a military sedan to the event. Where possible, General Mildren would always let me accompany him at events. I was sure he would not allow me to go with him this time. After we landed, his Aide-de-Camp told me to come with them, I did not want to fly with a co-pilot, the crew chief always flew in the co-pilots seat and I had taught him how to shut the aircraft down.

We arrived at the location, the Generals had lunch with the President in one room, and we had lunch in an adjoining area. At one point, I excused myself and went to the restroom and while turning at the end of the hallway, I actually bumped into Mrs. Kennedy; she was accompanied by her sister. I apologized to her and she said no problem. I have the beautiful luncheon program framed and hanging on my wall. On that fateful day, November 22, 1963, I spent most of the morning flying the General, went back to the airport, then went home to take a nap before returning to the Officer's Club to party. When I arrived at the club, the door was locked, since I knew there were some folks inside, I thought they had seen me drive up and locked the door as a joke. I pounded on the door for some time, the bartender came to the door and without opening it said that the club was closed, I said "Frantz, open the door, enough of the jokes." He opened the door and said that the General had closed all the clubs, I asked him why, and he replied that President Kennedy had been assassinated. It was a terrible blow to hear those words, a sad time indeed.

Fast forward to 1968, I was in Vietnam on my second tour stationed with the 1st Air Cavalry Division at Camp Evans. The phone rang one day and the Chief of Staff asked me if I knew General Mildren, I replied that I was his pilot in Germany. He told me to pack my bags, a plane would be there that afternoon to take me to Long Binh, as General Mildren requested my transfer. He was now a three star and I flew for him for almost a year. During that time, he asked me if I was a Regular Army Officer, I replied that I was not. He asked me if I was going to stay in the army, and when I replied that I was going to, he said we will put you in for a Regular Army Commission because when this war is over, there will be a severe reduction in force with a large percentage of the Officer Corps let go. He was absolutely correct, I would have been one of those had it not been for him. He was subsequently promoted to four stars; his concern for my career was instrumental in allowing me to retire after 20 years and eight months, doing something that I really loved. By the way the pilot of another Division Commander was none other than Kris Kristofferson, once he was flying his Commander to our Headquarters, accompanying him was my old classmate at ASU, Dallas Wood, now a retired Lt. Col. Dallas said the weather was so bad that he was sure they would certainly crash, but they made it. Dallas said when he stepped out of the Huey, his knees buckled and he hit the ground. He told Kris that he would never fly with him again. For you pilots, our weather minimums were clear of the clouds and ¼ mile visibility, which means you can fly anytime.

I had the opportunity to meet several VIPs during the time I flew General Mildren in Vietnam. Some of the more interesting folks, at least to me, were General Curtis LeMay, Billy Graham, Vickie Carr, Danny Kaye, Martha Raye, General Creighton Abrams, and later his son, Brigadier General Abrams, whom we invited to Atlanta to speak at the tribute to World War II veterans and another famous name in military history, Major General George Patton IV, the son of the famous World War II General George Patton, once on the battlefield near Long Binh and again in Atlanta when he spoke at a dedication ceremony sponsored by the Atlanta Vietnam Veterans Business Association, of which I am a member.

But the most interesting man I met and truly enjoyed was Tex Ritter. I watched him on TV and the movies as a kid, listened and loved his songs, especially "Cattle Call," "Rye Whiskey," "High Noon," "Boll Weevil" and "The Chisholm Trail." His band was called The Texans and he was simply the best and was loved and admired by all.

One night in 1968, I went to the Officers Club in Long Binh, just north of Saigon and found to my complete surprise that Tex Ritter was coming that evening and would be performing. I staked out a nice table near the stage and eagerly awaited one of my long-time heroes. He was introduced, came on stage with just his guitar and sang most of his great songs. One of the songs he sang was "Hillbilly Heaven" and I was, in fact, there.

After he performed, he came out and met some of us in the audience and much to my surprise, he sat down at my table and we visited for over thirty minutes. A very attractive nurse approached and asked Mr. Ritter if he wanted a drink, he thanked her and said no. About five minutes later she came back and asked again, this time Tex told her that he did not care for a drink and his tone indicated that he did not want to be asked again. Then he told us that he did have a drinking problem at one time, but had gone cold turkey and never had another drink. My respect and admiration for him only increased as a result of this incredible chance meeting.

After a few days of steady flying with the marshals and troops, we were given a day off. My hometown was not far from Millington, across the Mississippi River in Arkansas. I asked Gene if he wanted to fly with me to visit my Mom and other family members. We landed near my brother's home. I was flying and paying attention to my family on the ground and almost clipped the top of a tree on the banks of a river that ran in front of my brother's home. Later I mentioned it to Gene and he said, "I was watching the tree while you watched your family," that's what friends are for. We gave tours of the helicopter and everyone was sufficiently impressed.

My family's farm was several miles from there, I knew they would be working in the fields, so we decided to go over and check them out. My brother-in-law, Hoss Smith, who married my sister, Betty, was harvesting soybeans with a Combine and I lucked out, he was going away from us and did not see us approaching. I dropped down about 5 feet from the ground and slowed to a fast walk. The main rotor blades created a giant dust storm which looked like a tornado that blew out the sides of the chopper. I pulled up close behind the combine, finally Hoss saw the dust storm to his right and left, looked back and saw us right behind him, to say he was shocked would be an understatement. I flew home once more a few years later in a Beechcraft Baron, the Corvette of Beechcraft airplanes and had lunch with my Mom and brother Bob, who served in the Marine Corps and became the Superintendent of Valley View High School, which was, and still is one of the best schools in the state.

For the first time, I will share a story that Gene and I kept a secret during our time at and after our tour at Fort Benning. We were both going home for the Christmas holidays and Gene wanted to kill a deer and take the meat home to share with his family. There were lots of deer on the installation and he would go out hunting them, but could never get close enough to bag one. I said if you want one bad enough, we will get you one. He brought his rifle in one day, we cranked up the old H-34 and gave the rifle to the crew chief and told him to pick out a nice big buck and down him, which he did. Later that day, Gene went hunting again, lo and behold he bagged a large buck, that's our story and we're sticking to it.

We departed for home in Arkansas; he planned to spend a couple of days with me before going on to Abilene. My Dad and brothers always went hunting that time of year, but I would never go because my interest did not include sitting in the cold weather looking for deer. This time, I relented and off we went to a nice hunting lodge in South Arkansas. The dogs were running, doe season was in, and they picked out a nice log for me to sit on and within a half hour, I became very bored and started to take out the shells used for deer and put in some bird shot to kill a few squirrels.

I heard a noise, looked up and saw a doe, which I shot twice. While walking over, I heard another noise, looked over and saw a big buck. I killed it, then had to track down my nephew, Bud, and get his tag for that one. Had I known what was in store for me at deer camp, I would never had shot either one. Tradition here is to rub deer blood over one's face when they kill their first deer. I gave Gene one of the deer, because we ate his while there. I have never been deer hunting since then.

I retired from the Army in 1980; and moved to Atlanta, Georgia in 1981, a city I selected because I had lived there on two occasions and loved it. I had not married and had saved enough money to purchase a great bachelor house, build a pool and hot tub, grew a beard, and as almost all Vietnam Veterans, never discussed my military service because of the unpopular war and the public's reaction to it. The public had not separated the war from the warriors; and the Vietnam Veteran (average age 19.5) was never made to feel good about his military service. Consequently, they withdrew and suppressed their anger, and in a lot of cases, trauma. I didn't mind because my retirement salary and investments enabled me to live the life of Reilly, and I did so until October, 1982.

I was watching ABC's "Nightline" and they showed the Vietnam Veterans Memorial and talked about the dedication ceremonies on November 13, 1982. I was alone and suddenly became very emotional, the single most emotional experience of my life other than my Father's death. I realized that I *must* go to the dedication. I did not sleep at all that night. As events will show, I lost a lot of sleep the remaining three weeks.

The flooding of my emotions made me realize how angry a lot of Vietnam veterans were, especially those who were still suffering lingering problems as a result of their military service. All veterans who experience the horrors of war suffer to some degree from delayed stress. All other veterans returned home to family, peer and the public's support. The Vietnam veteran, the first teenage fought war, returned home to anger, ridicule and in many cases, hostility.

I knew the visit to the Vietnam Veterans Memorial could be a healing experience, and I started calling some of my friends to see if they wanted to go. Everyone I called said yes. The next night, I did not sleep much and during that time, I decided I had to do more. I was determined to get as many Vietnam Veterans to Washington, D.C. as possible.

I learned how to fly in college, flew for twenty years in the military, and was doing a little corporate flying in Atlanta in-between my vacations. Suddenly I knew a way--it was a long shot, but I knew I had to try.

Delta Airlines is headquartered in Atlanta, and I decided to attempt to lease an L-1011 jumbo jet capable of seating 300 people. I told a couple of friends and they laughed and said "Are you crazy? That's impossible! First of all, individuals do not charter planes from airlines; and furthermore, Delta would not even consider it!" After another sleepless night, I phoned the charter director for Delta, said I represented an organization, and that I wanted an appointment to discuss leasing an airplane. I got the appointment, thought up a name of an organization, and met with the Delta charter Director.

At first, he looked at me and I am sure he was thinking, "What kind of a screwball have we got here?" He could tell I was very serious about what I was saying, and I spent the next hour telling him about my plan. I convinced him I could fill the airplane, and with the help of donations from the public, I hoped I could reduce the fare considerably for the veterans. He never told me, but I am sure he was chuckling to himself. He was courteous, told me that Delta could not guarantee anything, but to keep him informed. He did not tell me what it would cost, and in my excitement, I forgot to ask. That shock would come later. At least, I was not turned down flat. I'm sure he considered the matter closed.

I walked out of Delta Headquarters, went to my car, unlocked it, and sat there for thirty minutes trying to figure out what the hell I should do next. I had a plan, I had the burning desire, but now I had exactly three weeks to accomplish the following:

1. Incorporate the 'Vietnam Special Flight, Inc.' with the State of Georgia.
2. Apply for non-profit, tax exempt status with the Internal Revenue Service in order to solicit donations.
3. Open an escrow account at a bank that would accept donations from the public.
4. Talk the public and the corporations of the Metro Atlanta area into donating monies.
5. Find 300 Vietnam veterans who wanted to go to Washington, D.C. for the Dedication Ceremonies of a Memorial that was mired deep in controversy. Many referred to it as 'the black wall of shame', and to further complicate the situation, it was

designed by an Oriental, a deep underlying factor that caused many to dislike it without knowing anything about it.

6. I had to pre-register the veterans prior to the flight, and had to find a location that would donate space large enough to handle the crowds.

7. Convince Delta Airlines to charter me an L-1011.

To make matters worse, I had to accomplish all this without a single contact. The only person I knew at this point was the Delta Charter Director, and I am sure he thought I was not playing with a full deck and that he would probably never see me again. As I sat there in my car right in front of Delta headquarters, I remembered the T.V. program and let it run through my mind again. Tears were streaming down my face, as they would many times again during the next few weeks.

It was a very busy place. I am sure people saw me, but I was oblivious to everything around me. When I finally returned to reality, my mind was made up; I would put everything I could into making this thing work!

I raced home; luckily I did not have an accident as I was trying to figure out what to do next. I knew my next step was the newspapers. I also had to refine my plan. Time was short, and Delta had told me they required the passengers to be pre-registered prior to the flight. Marriott had just built a large hotel near my home. It was close to the perimeter freeway that circles Atlanta, and it was easy to find. I called and asked if I could come by to look at meeting rooms for an organizational meeting. I walked in, asked for the Catering Manager, and told him the complete story. He liked the idea, discussed it with the Manager, and approved it. I emphasized the good publicity that the Marriott Corporation would receive, and I think that is why they went along with me. Rooms of the size we needed cost quite a lot and they did not charge me anything.

My next stop was the Atlanta Journal-Constitution, the only major newspaper serving the Atlanta area. They published a morning and evening edition.

I parked in a no-parking area, and took a deep breath before heading in. I had worn the best, most business-like suit I owned. I walked past the guard at the bottom floor, smiled, said hello, and got on the elevator acting as if I owned the place. Luckily, the floors were marked in the elevator, so I knew where to get off. I figured that the best place to start was with the managing editor. I stopped at the desk of a very nice looking lady and asked for the location of his office. As I was about to walk away, I remembered to ask her his name. She told me it was Edward Sears. I located his office, but he was out. I looked around the room and saw probably fifty people, some typing, some working on computers, and others talking about all kinds of stories. In short, it looked like a very busy, unorganized place. I found out later that was normal.

There were many unoccupied desks, so I walked over to one, sat down, and pretended to be writing something. About twenty minutes later, Mr. Sears walked into his office. I stood up, prepared myself for rejection, and walked into his office unannounced. I reached out my hand, shook his, introduced myself, and proceeded to tell him my story. By that time, I had it down pat and really did not give him a chance to tell me 'no' until I had finished. I finally stopped talking. He looked at me and said, "You've got my attention, now go tell it to the Assisting Managing Editor, Jim Stewart," and pointed back to another office. I thought to myself, 'Here goes, the old run around routine'. As I was leaving Mr. Sears' office, he told me that he was in the Army as a transportation officer, but did not serve in Vietnam. Jim Stewart, the man I was going to see, served in Vietnam. I said to myself, "I'll bet I'm one of the few people in this building that actually knows that they are Vietnam Veterans."

I walked back to the other office, and Mr. Stewart was out. I again sat down and acted like I knew what I was doing. I believe most of the reporters thought I worked there, or that I was looking for a job as most of them looked at me in a curious, quizzical way. Finally, Mr. Stewart walked into his office. I walked in, introduced myself, and told him that the Managing Editor had sent me back. I repeated my story again. He seemed interested, but I could not read him very well. At the end of the conversation, he called a reporter in and told him to take me down for a photograph. The photographer was an outgoing, friendly sort of fellow, and we hit it off immediately. He asked me what I was doing and I again told my story. He thought it was a great idea, and we started taking some photos. We were screwing around, joking, and it was a relief for me to be around someone who was not so serious and my normal character came out. I picked up a piece of cardboard and with a black felt-tip pen, wrote some numbers on it that resembled the ones you see on a police photo. He thought that was funny, and we proceeded to take a couple of pictures--front, side view, etc.

He said he would like to go on the flight, and I said I would invite a reporter and photographer from the newspaper to accompany the group. He liked the idea. I went back upstairs, said goodbye to Mr. Stewart, and thanked him for his assistance. I went home and waited for the big story--with my smiling face--to appear all over Atlanta the next morning.

In the morning, I rushed out to pick up the paper, and much to my surprise, no picture and a very short article concerning my efforts. They did publish a longer article in the evening edition, so I felt a little better. I never did know if my mug shots found their way to the managing editor. I trusted the photographer not to do that, but I never knew.

My next task was to convince the three local television stations to cover the story; and I struck pay dirt. The first station I called said they would like to come to my home and interview me. They had read the article in the newspaper, and thought it was a good story. The interview went well until the reporter started asking me why it was so important for me to go to the dedication. I told him that my best friend, someone who traveled around Europe with me chasing all the girls, was killed in Vietnam; and I wanted to honor him by going.

His death is another in a long list of stories in Vietnam that never got told. He was a gunship helicopter pilot and also a supply officer of a helicopter company. His replacement did not arrive in time to accomplish the transfer of all company supplies, worth millions. He could have left after his 365th day, but he extended his tour two weeks to help train his replacement. During the second week, one of his friends was shot down; and the Company Commander called for volunteers to go out and attempt to rescue the crew.

My friend Harry Whetzel volunteered to go and try to save his buddy's life. It was at night, and as they approached the area, the North Vietnamese were waiting. They waited until Harry attempted the rescue, and blew him out of the sky with a .50 caliber machine gun.

When I tried to tell that to the cameras, I broke down and they had to stop taping for awhile. I was embarrassed, but the reporter was very kind and told me not to apologize for the way I felt. After I had composed myself, we finished the taping. I asked him not to show the emotional part on television and he said O.K. It was going to be aired on the local news program that evening, and I fixed a drink, and sat down to watch my first appearance on television news.

The reporter was very nice to me, liked my story, and thought the idea of the flight was outstanding. He also knew how to cover a story. He left just enough of the emotional part in to make it a very moving piece of journalism. It worked. I started receiving all kinds of calls from Vietnam Veterans who wanted to know about the flight, and from people who wanted to know how to donate money for the trip.

Two days before, and as one of the conditions that Delta required, I had stopped in at the bank where I had recently transferred my checking account and talked them into opening an escrow account for the flight. All monies had to be mailed directly to the bank. I understood why Delta wanted this: they did not know me from anyone else, and wanted some kind of assurance that this was not some kind of flim-flam operation.

One of the reasons I selected the bank, was that it was completely staffed by good-looking women, and I never missed an opportunity to try and meet good-looking women. The bank manager, a very business-like individual, was not too crazy about the plan, but apparently she liked my idea and agreed to help.

The other television stations jumped on the bandwagon and came out to cover the story. By that time, the phone was ringing off the hook, and I had to get an answering service to take the calls while I was out meeting with other people.

Now it was time to incorporate the 'Vietnam Special Flight' and to apply for tax-exempt status. I lucked out again. My next door neighbor's wife was an attorney. I had become very good friends with Charlie and Diane House during the past year. We had several pool parties at my home together and had developed a good friendship. I called her at her office, told her what I was doing, and asked her for help. I gave her all the information over the telephone for the Articles of Incorporation, and told her that I needed it done yesterday, because I was soliciting donations as a non-profit, tax-exempt corporation. She said it was unusual to put the cart before the horse, but that she would do everything possible. She did, and after a few days, I was incorporated, the tax-exempt status would be temporary, with a final determination made by the IRS after a normal waiting period. The cost was $1,300.00 and they said they would bill me later, which was a relief for me, then came three shocks that made me realize that my friends may have been right in telling me that it was impossible.

I had set the wheels in motion with the media, incorporated the organization, and applied for tax-exempt status. My next step was to call Delta for our next meeting, and to get more information on the charter arrangements.

I called Delta, set up an appointment for the next day, and continued to answer the telephone. I arrived at Delta's office the next day, walked in, shook hands with Mr. Huckfeldt and received the three shocks.

The L-1011 would cost $43,950, we had to apply for an emergency waiver from the Civil Aeronautics Board, and the L-1011 could not land at National Airport in Washington, D.C. because of its size. We had to go into Baltimore-Washington Airport, over an hour away from D.C.

My heart almost stopped. I felt as if I was going to be sick, and I broke out in a cold sweat. I had talked the entire media establishment in Atlanta into covering the story. My phone was ringing off the hook, and I just received information that for all practical purposes shot my plans down in flames. I could see Mr. Huckfeldt talking, but I did not hear a word he said for a few minutes. My mind was filled with thoughts of having to cancel everything. I thought of what my friends would say. I would have to leave town for a few weeks on one of my vacations in order to avoid the humiliation. The flight was two weeks away, and I was sitting there numb.

I finally came to my senses as Mr. Huckfeldt passed an official looking document over for me to read. I could see the figure $43,950, and I could see the "X" marking the spot for my signature. I am sure he did not expect me to sign it. I immediately mustered my self-confidence, had no idea how I was going to accomplish it all, but picked up the document, pulled out my pen, and signed my name. I now personally owed Delta Airlines $43,950 for a contract on an L-10ll jumbo jet. I asked him what the first steps were in applying for the emergency waiver from the CAB. He did not know, but referred me to the Senior Attorney for Delta, Mr. Abramson. He called him and told him I was on the way over.

I walked into Mr. Abramson's office, introduced myself, and again repeated my story. He was very courteous, liked my idea, but did not hold out any hope of getting it accomplished. He personally worked up the waiver, called the CAB in Washington, D.C., and hand carried the waiver there himself. I was determined to continue. Somehow things had to work out.

Now I had to figure out how to get three-hundred people from the Baltimore-Washington Airport to Washington, D.C. I had talked to the folks who worked for the Vietnam Veterans Memorial Fund in

Washington before and I decided to call them for assistance. I finally talked to an individual on the transportation committee, but they did not have any kind of transportation, and could offer no recommendations. As the last resort, I asked for the number of a commercial bus line.

I contacted the Capitol Informer, a convention and concierge service, and lucked out. They still had coaches available at a cost of $2,695. I didn't know how I was going to get the $43,950 for the plane, but I told them to reserve the buses, and they did.

By now, I was having trouble sleeping, and I never had trouble sleeping before. As a matter of fact, I was known to sleep through mortar attacks in Vietnam. Then something happened that made my job a lot easier.

Ken Adams, an L-1011 pilot for Delta, called and said he was a Vietnam Veteran and wanted to meet me. He lived nearby and I told him to come by the next day. His brother also served in Vietnam, and had some very serious problems as a result. Ken wanted desperately to do something in memory of his brother, and he felt this was an excellent opportunity.

He told me he thought he could find the three pilots and the eleven flight attendants that would volunteer to work the charter on their day off; thereby reducing the cost of the plane.

I was ecstatic. After a few days, he called and told me that the crew was set. He came by my house often and provided me with a great deal of encouragement. He also said that he would try and get Delta to pay for the fuel and would also ask Delta to talk to the caterers in hopes they would donate the meals. After the President of Delta heard about the flight crew and other requests, he passed the word down that Delta would charter the plane to me at cost: $23,500. That was one happy moment and I did manage to get a few hours sleep that night; but it was not to last.

The next day I went by the bank. It had been a week since the story broke, and I expected a few thousand dollars in the account. As a matter of fact, Delta had asked me what would happen if we collected more money than needed. I had not considered that possibility, but immediately said any excess funds would be used to erect a monument or plaque in Atlanta in memory of those Georgians killed or missing in action during the Vietnam War. This information was also included in the Articles of Incorporation. I walked up to the desk of the good-looking lady that was handling the escrow account. I smiled, said hello and asked her for the total amount. She opened her folder, looked at it, and said $236. It was one helluva shock, and she sensed my reaction. She was very nice and said it was probably a little early yet.

I knew that I was again in trouble, and immediately started to think of ways to increase the donations. I had hoped that the public would respond in large numbers with small amounts, but now I had to look at other possibilities.

Lockheed-Georgia, headquartered in Atlanta, Georgia, made the L-1011 and they are one of this nation's largest defense contractors. Lockheed made millions of dollars off the Vietnam War; I called, explained the circumstances, and asked for a donation. Mr. Lee Rogers, the Special Assistant to the President was out of town, and no one else could make the decision. Finally he returned; Lockheed donated $1,000 to the trip.

Someone who worked for Georgia Power Company said they hired a lot of veterans. I took a chance, called and wrote them a letter. Georgia Power came through with a $1,000 donation.

One of the most satisfying donations came from Salomon Brothers, an investment firm. They collected $1,000 from their employees, called and said it was on the way. Things were looking up; but I still had a long way to go. The registration was scheduled in two days, and we still did not have much money.

I sat down and tried to think of another way to capture the public's attention. I thought if I could get an important politician to agree to go, it would help. Who was the most important politician in Georgia? Former President Jimmy Carter!

I called the President's office, discussed it with his Chief of Staff. He was interested and said he would let me know. A few days later, he told me they were considering going and would need six or eight seats, and told me to come by the office later and discuss the arrangements. I started telling everyone that we had a special guest signed up, but that I could not discuss it further, under orders from Carter's office. I told Ken Adams, the Delta pilot, and he and I went down to the Richard B. Russell Federal Building, passed through the security screening device, and went up to Carter's office. Let me tell you, former President's live very well.

He had a very nice office suite that was exquisitely decorated. We met with his Chief of Staff, and briefed him on the flight. I never knew why President Carter backed out, but we received word later that he could not join us due to a schedule conflict. I received a nice letter dated November 11, two days before the flight with these handwritten comments from the President: "Ron, I hope your trip was successful and meaningful. All of us owe you and the Vietnam Veterans a great deal of gratitude." I never knew his reasons for not going. It could have been security precautions or something else.

My twenty years in the military basically shielded me from the political world, and I did not know how damaging President Carter was to the military and veterans. He almost destroyed the military and for some reason did not care much for veterans either. Standard protocol for Presidents of the past was to meet with the National Commanders of the major veteran service organizations at the White House. Carter did not do that and one year the National Commander of the Veterans of Foreign Wars was from Georgia.

Looking back, I am very happy he did not go with us on the flight. Sometime God does indeed work in mysterious ways.

I cannot list other donors, there were many; but only small amounts. I appreciated them all. One came from Florida. After the flight, I sent a handwritten note to everyone who donated any amount. It was that important to me.

Now I faced the next effort: to pre-register the veterans. I was convinced I would get the three-hundred veterans easily, and I had calculated I would have to charge them $98.00 each for the round-trip airfare, coach buses and organizational expenses.

All three television networks responded again with the registration at the Marriott, and I even arranged for a small band from Fort McPherson, Georgia to entertain the vets. Several of my friends and their wives volunteered to help out. It was cold and rainy the morning of November 6, and the band had to cancel. That was the beginning of another bad day. The meeting room could handle about seventy at a time and our plan was to brief the vets in groups. Two television stations showed up for the first group, and things were going very smooth until I told them the donations were coming in very slow, and that I would have to charge $98 to cover the cost of the charter. A couple of vets expressed their displeasure; and one lady, the wife of a Vietnam veteran who had been experiencing difficulties, objected to the cost and started crying. I immediately saw that she could create a lot of problems, not only with the other veterans, but with the press. I told her not to worry, if they did not have the money, she could still go. She calmed down and things went smoothly again.

The next shock occurred when the room did not fill up the second time. At the end of the day, only one-hundred twenty-two veterans had signed up, with only about thirty paying the $98.00.

A girlfriend had been helping me with the paperwork, telephones, and other things. She and I went home and I fixed a strong drink and tried to recover. All my outward signs to everyone else did not indicate any problems with the flight. She knew different, and provided me with a lot of support. I will forever be grateful to her for all her assistance and encouragement.

I had one week to solve this new dilemma. One thing I could do was ask Delta to charter a smaller aircraft. That would cut the cost of the bus transportation. All I had to do was convince the veterans to walk from National Airport to the Monument, which is about five miles. I did not want to alarm Mr. Huckfeldt at Delta, so I called Jim Hufferrnan, his assistant. He and I got along very well and I felt I could level with him.

I called, told him about the low turnout, and asked if I could get a smaller airplane. He reminded me that the crew had been selected for the L-1011, and that they may not have anything smaller. That sick feeling came over me again. He was upbeat, and tried to encourage me as much as possible. I told him not to tell Mr. Huckfeldt and that I would come up with something.

The television coverage of the registration helped. We started receiving additional money, small amounts, and veterans began calling again. Now I had to fill the L-1011. I was determined to do it even if I had to make up the difference myself, which at this time amounted to around $15,000. I decided the only way I could get more veterans was to tell everyone who called that they could go, regardless of their ability to pay. I also asked them to call every Vietnam Veteran they knew and to tell them about the flight. I also began calling everyone I knew and asked them personally to go. Three of my good friends, who I worked with in Atlanta, had retired from the Army and agreed to go and help out. Sgt. Maj. Bledsoe, MSGT Wolfe and MSGT Mullins were a great help during the flight.

Now I had five days, and things began picking up. I called one of my best friends, who was the Professor of Military Science and Tactics at the University of San Francisco, and asked him to come to Atlanta and help me with the flight.

Since I chartered the plane, it was also my responsibility to issue the tickets and check the passengers on board at the gate. I wanted my friend, LTC Russ Calvert, to assist me at the check-in and during the flight. I knew the press would be there and much of my time would be taken up with them and also answering questions from the passengers.

On top of everything else, the emergency waiver at the Civil Aeronautics Board in Washington was going nowhere. The senior attorney at Delta had done all he could, and gave me the name of the individual at the CAB. I had talked to her once, and she told me she was considering the application. The next time I called, she was out of town, and no one else could take action. It was now three days before the flight, and I finally made contact and convinced her that a decision had to be made NOW. She said to call the next day. I did, and she informed me that the waiver was approved. At last, the final obstacle had been removed. If the waiver had been disapproved, I think I would have left the Country.

Next came the final hurdle, Delta informed me that the money had to be paid prior to the flight. The donations had picked up, but nowhere near the amount needed. Many of the veterans who were going to pay would be bringing the money to the check-in gate. I had not been told earlier that the money had to be paid prior to the flight

My brother-in-law, Mr. Billy McCoy, who was President of Reagan Commerce Bank in Houston, Texas, came to my rescue. I called him, told him the story, and informed him that Delta Airlines needed $23,500 wired to their account forty-eight hours prior to the flight. He drafted a personal loan for that amount, mailed it to me, and wired the sum to Delta immediately.

At last, all requirements were satisfied. Now I had two days to fill the plane. I forgot about the money and concentrated on preparing for the flight. The idea to ask the veterans to call their friends paid off. The phone rang most of the last day and until midnight the night prior to the flight. Another reason the calls picked up was the national coverage of the five-day tribute that began on November 10. President Reagan attended the round-the-clock reading of the nearly 58,000 names of those killed or missing in Vietnam. That coverage by the national media and other coverage of the events caused my telephone to ring constantly.

My friend arrived from California the night prior to the flight. I briefed him on the check-in procedures, and got to bed around 1:00 a.m. We left for the airport at 6:00 a.m. for the 9:00 a.m. departure. We had six seats left, it was unbelievable. The money was still a problem, but I could not believe I had overcome all the other obstacles.

I had given everyone a hand-out detailing all the information on the flight. At the bottom of the hand-out, I had written: "Remember: When all is said and done, these men and women we are going to honor, have paid the ultimate sacrifice to the service of their Country when asked, and God graces their soul for doing so."

As I said earlier, I shed a lot of tears during this period of time, but none were due to the problems with the flight.

I answered the phone one day, and it was a father of a Vietnam Veteran who had suffered severe emotional problems as a result of his Vietnam experience, and he wanted his son to go. While I was talking to him, my phone clicked (I had the call waiting feature). I put the father on hold and answered the other line. It was the mother of the same Vietnam Veteran. She was at work and decided to call. I was already in tears from the other conversation, and she proceeded to tell me the same story about her son. It was a story that I was to hear again and again.

One black lady called and asked me if I could take a photograph of her son's name and send it to her when I returned. She said she loved her son more than anything, and he volunteered to serve this Country and died so young. She was not bitter and said he knew the dangers, but would do it again. I told her that I would try my best. The crowds were so large that it was impossible for anyone, other than immediate family members of those listed on the Wall, to get near it. When I returned, I called her, told her that I could not get the photograph, but assured her that I would be going again and I would bring it back for sure. She called me a few days later and told me her relatives had seen how much she wanted to go, and they were going to take her. She was extremely nice and told me that she was grateful for all I had done. It was another of those phone calls that caused me to become very emotional again.

Another remarkable story came out of this flight. Tom Carter of Gainesville, Georgia, called me one evening and said he had about 26 Vietnam Veterans coming over with him to go on the flight. His remarkable story centered around the Duff family, who live in that area. Their son, Phillip Duff, was killed in Vietnam. His wife had moved in with them, and she had a son, a son that had never seen or known his dad. They could not afford the cost of the flight, and Tom Carter and his friends raised the money for their tickets. They were the nicest, most pleasant family you could ask for.

They were extremely grateful for the chance to go to Washington to visit the Memorial. I had arranged for two television crews to go along on the flight, for a donation of course. The Duffs were very cooperative, and their interviews were very moving and something everyone will always remember. This is another story of the Vietnam Veteran which is seldom ever told.

There are countless stories that can be told about the flight, like the big, burly, black man getting off the plane in Atlanta. He came up to me with tears in his eyes, reached in his pocket, pulled out a card, handed it to me and said: "Ron, if you ever need anything, and I mean *anything*, all you have to do is call that number." It was a very moving moment, and I shall never forget him. I still have his card.

Another story that completely caught me off guard and was something that never occurred to me, I received a call from a Vietnam Veteran from LaGrange, Georgia. He had been severely wounded and medically discharged. He had also been a German Sheppard police dog handler. All the dogs were trained at Fort Benning, Georgia, and they shipped hundreds to Vietnam to be used to sniff out explosives and booby traps. But the most shocking thing he told me was they had to be left behind when we departed Vietnam because of the dangers of spreading diseases in the United States.

He said many Vietnam Veterans owed their lives to those dogs, and he wanted to get one from Fort Benning and take it along on the flight to represent all the dogs left behind. It's hard to say what happened to those poor animals. Without a doubt, many, and maybe all, have been killed and very possibly eaten by now. He was emotional about it, and I agreed without checking with Delta. Later I called Delta and they told me the dog could be caged and would have to ride in the baggage compartment. The G.I. had made a real nice blanket for him with patches and had it fitted around his body. The dog was the center of attention with everyone at the check-in counter, including the press. When we got ready to depart, the dog came on the aircraft with us, to the cheers of everyone.

At around 7:30 a.m., the corridors of the airport began humming with the noise of large groups of people, all talking at the same time. Our gate was at the end of a concourse.

It was a large area, and it rapidly began to fill up. Many of the veterans wore their old Army jackets, their flop hats, and other military paraphernalia. You could close your eyes and it sounded like the airport in Saigon.

These were the lucky ones: they survived, just as they had survived in the corridors of the airport in Saigon. Some were friends, others were strangers meeting new friends. It was an incredible experience, but nothing compared to what was corning up.

The press were everywhere; two television crews would take the flight with us. Many radio stations and the print media were interviewing just about anyone who wanted to talk. The dog handler must have given ten separate interviews; everyone loved his story.

Here they were, the Vietnam Veterans, the one group of veterans who served their country well; the veteran who <u>never</u> lost a major battle in Vietnam, but was made to feel that what they did was wrong. Here they felt wanted; here they shared a common feeling, a common bond; in short, a brotherhood.

We checked everyone on board, and had eight seats left. Many wives and family members were standing there waiting for the departure. I asked if anyone wanted to go. I immediately got eight volunteers, and I told them to come aboard. They were eight of the happiest people I have ever seen.

We taxied out to the runway, took off, and as the plane lifted off the runway, everyone on board cheered just as they did on every freedom bird flight that left Saigon. It had been 12 years since I left Saigon on the next to last aircraft after the peace accords were signed, and I remembered it as if it were yesterday.

But this was a different flight. This was to be a flight of discovery; it was to be an extraordinary flight. I wish my command of the English language would permit me to relay to the reader how much this flight would mean to everyone on board.

I was going to pay my respects, to honor one of the best friends of my life. My good friend, Marilyn Weitzel, was sending her 16-year old son whose father was killed in Vietnam. The Duffs were going to meet with the soul of their son, husband, and father. Almost everyone on that plane had an individual story to tell. Ken Adams, the L-1011 pilot who was a great help to me and who felt that this was one way to honor his brother. I found out that his wife was celebrating her birthday, and Ken had slipped a cake, with candles on board. He gave me the high sign, I announced over the plane's intercom system that we had a birthday, and three-hundred happy folks sang happy birthday to her at 25,000 feet. The crusty L-1011 Captain who had been a pilot during World War II and had flown countless combat missions was at home with us.

The veterans were unaware that the pilots and the flight attendants had volunteered to fly this charter at no cost and on their day off. I announced this fact over the intercom system, and the group responded with thundering applause.

Then a strange thing began to occur as we got closer to Washington: the noise level began to subside. The closer we got, the quieter it became. I could sense they were becoming anxious, as if they were about to experience the unknown. They became more reflective, many staring out the aircraft windows.

We landed, and three-hundred Vietnam Veterans walked thru the corridors of the Baltimore-Washington Airport with their heads held high. I had brought an American and a Georgia flag with us, and asked two of my good friends, Sergeant Major Carl Bledsoe and Master Sergeant Tom Mullins, who served with me for three years in Atlanta, if they would carry the flags. It was a small way for me to honor two of the most capable soldiers that I had the honor to meet during my 20-year career.

Everyone in the airport stopped in their tracks. Some gave us the thumbs up sign. A few even gave us a hand. It was a very good feeling. For some, it was the first time anyone had publicly expressed their thanks, and some of the guys became a little misty-eyed.

We arrived at the mall area, formed up--flags in front--and began moving toward the monument.

I moved to an area where I could get an unobstructed view of the Wall. I was standing at an angle, and looked at it for a long time. The first thing I wanted to do was find my friend's name; but it was impossible. The only people that could get that close were immediate members of the families of those brave souls whose names will be forever etched on a memorial to their supreme sacrifice.

Then it was time for the speeches. They were all good, and very moving, but the one that is forever etched in my mind was delivered by Mrs. Helen J. Stuber, President of the Gold Star Mothers. She said, "My son, Dan joined the United States Marines in August of 1966. He felt it was his duty as an American citizen to serve his Country in the Armed Forces. I have no feeling of bitterness, for it was his decision and his alone to join the United States Marine Corps." As his mother, if my son had to be taken, I thank the Good Lord that he stood for our great Country and not against it. I am so grateful, after all these years, that our Country is pausing today and all these last few days, to honor the Vietnam Veterans in our nation's capitol for their welcome home they never received." The ceremonies were over. We boarded the buses and headed for the airport for the trip home.

On the flight back, someone asked if he could say a prayer over the intercom. It was a very moving moment. He gave thanks for the healing process that occurred, he gave thanks for the ones who survived, and prayed for those whose names were listed on the Wall.

The door to the plane opened up. I walked out, turned around, and said goodbye to each of my new friends. There were handshakes, hugs, thumbs up, and tears. I said goodbye to the crew and headed for my car. Some wanted to stop for drinks on the way home. I was emotionally and physically exhausted, begged off, and went home and, for the first time in three weeks, got a good night's sleep.

The next morning, my phone rang. I picked up the receiver and a voice said, "I never felt like I came home from Vietnam until we landed in Atlanta last night. Thank you and God bless you." He hung up and I sat there with tears running down my face.

I can tell you that the five-day national tribute and the dedication ceremonies of the Vietnam Memorial were the beginning of the healing process for a lot of Vietnam Veterans. I have included a couple of the letters from some of the veterans and their families, but the one I liked very much is from the wife of a Vietnam Veteran, JoAnne Harris.

"Ron, this note is just to say a word of thanks from one of the wives of a Vietnam veteran that you made it possible to go on the flight to Washington last Saturday. Words can't express what that day meant to me, and I'm sure to my husband. I have never felt so close to him in the past almost twelve years. Again, I would like to say thanks for your efforts and concerns. Yours truly, JoAnne Harris."

It is difficult to describe to anyone who is not a Vietnam Veteran what happened that day. There were thousands of veterans who had suppressed their feelings and their emotions for so long, and now this Wall caused them to release a lot of the anger, a lot of hurt, and above all, it gave them the opportunity to embrace each other in a mutual bond. Friendships were made that day that will last forever.

Family members would walk up to the Wall, reach out and touch a name, running their fingers back and forth. To them, they were touching their loved one. And as I found out during a later visit, you can see a reflection of yourself, and it is somehow comforting. People talk to the names, some leave flowers, some write personal notes and letters and either place them next to the name or at the base. There were letters that are very personal, some that only make sense to the writer and the name. Many Vietnam veterans leave a hat, a jacket and other personal items behind. To me, it is an affirmation that they have been there. They treat the name as a body, and they leave something to somehow let them know that they care; that they will always care; that they will never forget them.

I think I know why this phenomenon happens. The surviving Vietnam Veterans know in their hearts and soul that what they did was honorable. The men and women whose names appear on the Wall will never know how the American people have honored them. So we honor them in our own special way: we visit them, we talk to them, and we leave things for them. I received this note and a small donation. It read: "To whoever you are, I have no family involved in the Vietnam War, but to paraphrase Ernest Miller Hemingway, "Go not to see for whom the bell tolls-it tolls for thee. Enjoy and God Bless. Sincerely, Verna D. Blackstock"

On the flight back, one of my friends, Mr. Richard Grant, announced over the aircraft intercom that "The Vietnam Special Flight" was still short of money. Someone passed the hat and $968.00 was collected and passed back to me. You do not expect things like that to happen, and if caught me off guard again--more tears.

It is with great satisfaction to announce that because of all the special people in Georgia, the corporations, friends and family, I was able to raise enough money so that 202 Vietnam Veterans went on the trip FREE; 95 vets paid $98.00 for round-trip airfare and bus transportation. All this was made possible by the generous act of people helping other people, which included friends like Ben Sharp and Murel Williams, my classmates from West Ridge, Arkansas, and countless other Americans, known only to themselves, who cared about the Vietnam Veteran.

Several days after the flight, I received the following letter in the mail. I cannot begin to tell you how humble it made me feel to receive this "thank you" from a fellow Vietnam Veteran. I will cherish it forever.

November 20, 1982

Dear Ron,

The common man longs to make his mark on the world by giving and leaving something of himself which will last on into perpetuity. The uncommon man completes the act which does so and then turns his head and unassumingly ignores the praise which he is given and so richly deserves.

Ron, you have made a lasting impression on me and at least 289 or so lives for the journey you created last Saturday. It was a journey of renewal and restoration of a faith too long forgotten. You brought a group of individuals to that much needed catharsis.

I shall be ever grateful for having been a part of such an historic event. I am equally as grateful to have been blessed to be brought to such an experience by an uncommon man. Thank you!

Most Sincerely,
Dan Lorton

This will probably be the high point of my life. I know I have never experienced anything quite like it before, and doubt if I ever will again.

When I organized the flight, I had fears of my telephone ringing off the hook with crank calls and calls from people who still had anti-war and anti-Vietnam Veteran sentiments. Much to my surprise, I did not receive a single negative phone call.

The "Welcome Home" that the Vietnam Veterans experienced and finally received can be largely attributed to the efforts and concerns of President Ronald Reagan and his Administration. During his first four years, he established the Vietnam Veterans Leadership Program, with fifty volunteer organizations in forty-six states. In addition, he signed legislation ensuring employment and training opportunities for Vietnam Veterans. The Small Business Administration set aside over $50 million for direct loans.

But most importantly, he gave the Vietnam Veteran what he wanted the most—a feeling that what we did was deserving of the honor that other veterans have received. Through his efforts, the State and Federal Governments, and more importantly, the public have expressed their appreciation to the Vietnam Veteran.

After ten long and sometimes bitter years, the Vietnam Veterans are now receiving the long awaited "Welcome Home."

"HOME AT LAST"

A few days after the flight, I sent the President of Delta Airlines a letter of appreciation, I have included my letter and his response.

Several people, some in the media, suggested I send this story to 20/20 in hopes they would tell the story to the national public. I forwarded the part about organizing the flight to Mr. Av Westin, Vice President of ABC News. I received a prompt reply with assurances that they would consider it. Sometime later, I was told Mr. Westin had been promoted to another position in ABC, apparently his successor was not as enthusiastic as Mr. Westin. I have included Mr. Westin's letter of February 21, 1985.

And now, it was vacation time again, and I intended to pick up where I had left off a month before. Much to my surprise, events during the next two months would overtake me again.

In December, 1982, one month after the flight, I received a telephone call from a representative of ACTION, the national volunteer agency.

President Reagan had signed legislation in November, 1981 that created the Vietnam Veterans Leadership Program, a program that would establish a federal grant initiative in each state. Its purpose was to draw volunteers from successful Vietnam Veterans in the community to assist those veterans who may still be experiencing difficulties as a result of their service.

I had no intention of getting involved, and I wasted no time in letting them know. I did agree to find someone for them. They needed a full-time Executive Director and a non-paid Chairman of the Board of Directors. Both of these positions would, in effect, be appointees of the Reagan Administration.

I received a detailed briefing about the purposes of the organization and how the other VVLP's were established. The Georgia VVLP would be the 41st of the planned fifty nationwide.

I had met Keegan Federal, Jr., a Superior Court Judge, a few months before the flight on a sailboat at Lake Lanier. We were crewing a friend's sailboat, and it was quite obvious that neither he nor I knew anything about sailing. The blow-boaters are a strange breed of folks. My idea of a good time on the lake is to get a few girls, some eats, drinks and music, drop anchor, and enjoy. Their main function in life is to beat the other boats in a race, then spend the remaining hours in the day explaining how they did it.

Judge Federal went on the flight with me, and I asked him if he would consider the Chairman's position. I continued to look for a director. The more I talked about the job, the more interesting it sounded.

In effect, we would be our own boss, and the program could be what we wanted it to be. I set up a meeting with a representative from Washington and several prominent Vietnam Veterans. The representative could only make it to Atlanta during the week that I had scheduled one of my vacations. I told him that I could not make it, but that I had arranged for several Vietnam Veterans to meet with him.

I left for Aspen, Colorado and a week on the slopes. I had a great time, but could not get the idea of the appointment out of my mind. After seven glorious days and nights, I returned to Atlanta and talked to some of the guys who had met with Mr. Moorefield. They were very excited about the program, and I finally did what I did not want to do. I called Washington, and told Mr. Moorefield to please consider me for the job of Executive Director. They did, Judge Federal and I were confirmed at a meeting in Washington, D.C., in January, 1983.

I could not believe myself. Now I had the responsibility of creating an organization from scratch. Judge Federal was a great help in lining up the Board of Directors. He knew five outstanding Vietnam Veterans, and I found six more. Now we had a good Board of Directors, no office, and if you can believe it, my first two tasks were to form an organization and apply for a non-profit, tax- exempt status.

No problem. I took the paperwork from "The Vietnam Special Flight," changed the wording somewhat, and saved $1,300.

Now I needed office space. We could probably move into a governmental building downtown. Atlanta was, and still is, in the process of reworking the city's freeway system. Several years ago, some bright traffic engineer decided it would be nice to converge two major interstate systems in downtown Atlanta--Interstates 75 and 85--major thoroughfares to Florida and Alabama. With the construction, it would take me a couple of hours in traffic.

Fate was riding with me again. One of my friends, Phillip Darnell, knew an attorney who had office space in a new office complex only ten minutes from my house, and he could not find anyone to share the cost.

Through a series of financial arrangements, I now had a beautiful office with a magnificent view. Michael Mantegna, a combat veteran, donated the space to the program. His generosity is only the beginning of the great things that happened to me and the Georgia Vietnam Veterans Leadership Program.

I had the good fortune to meet Mr. Tommy Clack, a triple amputee, no legs and one arm, who is the special assistant to the Director of the VA Medical Center in Atlanta, and a human dynamo. Tommy is handicapped in name only. In my opinion, he stands as tall as any man I have ever met. Not only did he help me with the members of the Board of Directors, but he introduced me to Georgia's Commissioner of Veterans Affairs, Mr. Pete Wheeler, who would be one of our strongest supporters when we needed assistance.

My philosophy is, "Do not waste time. If you want something, go for it. The only thing they can do is turn you down."

I asked the Governor of Georgia, Joe Frank Harris, for a grant to hire an employment director. I got it, and hired Mr. Arthur Hamilton, who turned out to be a superb choice.

In a little over a year, Tony found 394 full-time, meaningful jobs for Vietnam Veterans. Also, we were able to convince the Veterans Administration to give us an employment office in their Vet Center, which is located in a central location easily reached by the vets.

Next, Mr. Andrew Farris, a member of our Board of Directors, found out that the United States Small Business Administration had set aside $25 million for direct loans to Vietnam veterans. The program had not been publicized; so Andy contacted some of his friends in the business world and they decided to set up a class at the Vet Center and to explain to the veterans how to fill out the loan application packet. Our first class was taught in a small meeting room to eight Vietnam Veterans.

We are now on our fourth series of fourteen seminars that are taught two nights a week at Georgia State University. The first night, we had 85 Vietnam veterans; the series prior to that had 186 vets enrolled. Mr. Clarence Barnes, District   Director of the Atlanta SBA office, opened up the last two series.

Andy received the U.S. Small Business Administration's National Veterans Advocate Award for 1984. Andy and the GVVLP were honored in Washington, D.C. at an awards banquet. He was also given the honor of placing a wreath at the Vietnam Veterans Memorial and a personal meeting with President Reagan.

The GVVLP submitted a grant request to the SBA office in Washington for a one-year grant of $59,000 to hire Andy full-time and to video tape the seminars in order to outreach the State of Georgia and nine (9) major cities in the United States. The grant was approved; we have completed the taping and have met with much success in Columbus, Savannah, and Gainesville, Georgia.

During the past eleven months, 154 Vietnam veterans applied for an SBA loan; 100 were approved for $15.3 million.

That was quite a jump from an eight-man class in the attic of the Vet Center. Nine of the fourteen instructors in the free workshops are combat Vietnam veterans who donated their time and expertise in order to help their fellow veterans.

Our last, and by no means less important, area of interest is improving the public's image of the Vietnam Veteran. Unfortunately, the media played a large part in stereotyping the Vietnam veteran. He was pictured as a drug-crazed, baby killer who should be watched at all times.

The vast majority of Vietnam Veterans adapted well back into their home environments, and never experienced any difficulties. There was a lot of suppressed anger, and it has surfaced from time to time in a small percentage of the vets.

All combat veterans of all wars suffer from stress. Almost all other veterans received support from governmental agencies, peer groups, friends, and family. Unfortunately, the Vietnam veteran was made to feel that he accomplished nothing; he lost the war; and to the dismay of the veteran, had to take the blame.

It took ten years, but the public finally separated the war from the warrior. The five-day national tribute and the dedication of the Vietnam Memorial was the beginning back for us.

As a result, I had very few problems in organizing the following events. These events were set up to honor the veterans and their service to their Country. It also gave the veteran a chance to come out and rejoin society, a society that now understood.

Our first special day was on July 4, 1983. Mr. Ted Turner and the Atlanta Braves dedicated a baseball game to the Vietnam Veteran. I bugged our National Office until we got a personal two-minute tape from President Reagan. It was a superb tape that was a tremendous boost to our young program.

Mr. Turner liked it so much that he had it shown on the large stadium TV screen for two nights. It was also aired over CNN cable TV to over 25 million households and broadcast to sixty-three regional radio stations. While coordinating the event, I met Bob Larsen, who operated the stadium matrix board. He agreed to flash a message on the screen at periodic intervals urging the local business community to hire Vietnam Veterans. The response was great, and Bob has been running the spots at every Atlanta Braves and Falcons game since that time at no charge.

Our next event was to be held at Six Flags over Georgia, a large amusement park in Atlanta. Ms. Marilyn Weitzel worked for the U.S. Army Recruiting Command, and she arranged for a parachute free-fall team, the Silver Wings from Fort Benning, Georgia, to jump into a lake at the park. In addition, we had the Army's newest Blackhawk helicopter on display. We also made space available for Vietnam Veterans to display their arts and crafts, and had a local band to entertain.

The response was so great that we were asked to do it again the following year.

Next, I approached Mr. Turner and the Atlanta Hawks to dedicate a basketball game with the Boston Celtics. They agreed. We were able to talk Mr. James Brown, the godfather of soul, into singing the National Anthem. I was a little concerned about him forgetting the words and asked the public relations folks at the Hawk's office to make sure the words were displayed on the screen. That was no problem. He did it acappella, and it was great. He brought the house down!

We also had a chorus group of young men from the 82d Airborne entertain and the audience response was outstanding. Another special event, and the most spectacular, was with the Atlanta Falcons. The Golden Knights are the Army's world famous parachute free fall jump team. They travel the world in support of major events. Their schedule is set up a year in advance. I called the Atlanta Falcons, and asked them if they were interested in dedicating a game to the Vietnam Veteran. I told them that we could possibly get the Golden Knights. The Falcons schedule was not due in for approximately four more months, and we had to guess at a date. They knew they were going to play an afternoon game with the Houston Oilers sometime in September, so we selected September 23rd and submitted it to the Golden Knights. Luck was riding with us again. When the Falcons schedule was released, that was indeed a home game.

I submitted the letter to the Atlanta-Fulton County Stadium Authority for permission to jump into the stadium. We were turned down. We made contact with State Senator Leroy Jenkins, who heads the Authority, and I received permission after we had secured approval from the police department and Mayor Andrew Young's office.

The jump was the highlight of the day. The first jumper came into the stadium with a large American flag; the second had the game ball. The last three jumpers were hooked up until about fifteen feet above the ground. The crowd went wild. We presented the game ball to the Falcons owner, Mr. Rankin Smith, Sr. He was simply delighted at the show, and I am sure we will be back again next year.

I thought I would include a letter that was written by my oldest sister, Elaine Miller McCoy during my second tour in Vietnam in 1968. I was stationed at Camp Evans, the home of the 1st Air Cavalry Division. Camp Evans was located in the northern part of South Vietnam and was heavily involved in the TET Offensive, the battle that changed the course of the war. When Walter Cronkite remarked that, "This war cannot be won," was the beginning of the end. This is the letter my Sister wrote at the time:

"Ron--I just wanted to tell you a few things I have had on my mind. We cannot possibly imagine what all happened in Vietnam, one of the most senseless wars with much death and terrible times. I did want to say that you had our prayers. When Mom would get a letter from you she would write on it some and send it to me. Mom, Marsha and I prayed over ever letter.

One day I heard over the TV that Camp Evans was completely destroyed. It being prayer service, Billy and I went and prayed for you. Thank God Mom did not hear about Camp Evans being destroyed. It was several days later, I called Mom, dreading something had happened to you. Just that day she heard from you. Thank God. No one except you and your crew know and saw what a terrible time spent there, all for nothing, death and sorrow. The things you had to do--you did it--some I knew and some I cannot even imagine them, death and destruction.

I believe you only survived because of much thoughts and prayers. I cannot imagine the worry and heartache with Mom---I cannot think of one of my boys living through war. I just had you on my mind and you called this day, I told you we are still praying for you.--Love, Elaine, Billy and kids."

Now for the first time, I will share with my family what happened to me at Camp Evans. A few days before the attack, my eyes begin to bother me. It became obvious that one was infected and the Battalion Flight Surgeon told me to go to the Hospital in DaNang and see the Ophthalmologist. He informed me that I had Uveitis, a serious infection of the inner eye. He also informed me that I might have to be med-evaced to Japan. Two days later, my eye seemed to be getting worse, the Doctor told me that he had a strong medicine and asked for my approval to use it. With the pain level, I told him, of course. It was steroids and it knocked out the infection quickly and I departed DaNang by helicopter to Camp Evans.

The attack had hit the Division ammo dump and caused tremendous damage to the base camp, the day before the attack, our Battalion had 42 helicopters, after the attack we had two that were flyable, they were flying during the attack. My small tent was completely destroyed, the only thing that survived was a metal jewelry box and it was burned.

The prayers of my family did indeed work. A few days later I wrote this poem:

WHY THE GUNS

The tent is cold and wet
I am miserable, so distressed
Why the guns
The music plays
The news is bad
Why the guns
The nations argue like kids over toys
But I have seen the toys die
A dirty, rotten, smelly death
Why the guns
They praise the soldiers
Some spit at him, call him names
All in the same breath
Why the guns
The campaign begins
Candidates shout, peace, peace
The people agree
The soldier, above all agrees
He knows why
Why the guns
Why the guns
The night erupts
Shells bursts, men scream
You pray, why me
The knife of pain
The night is cold, dark, alone
Death
Death is my peace
They shout peace, peace
Why the guns
Why the guns
Why the guns

Written at 1ˢᵗ Air Calvary Division, Camp Evans, South Vietnam, May 1968.

As I mentioned in the forward, I have been surprised, excited and blessed by the many riches that have come my way, all because I wanted to be of service to a group of Veterans, the Vietnam Veteran, who did not receive the grateful thanks of the Nation that was accorded all the Veterans that came before us. The Korean Veterans will tell you that they were also the forgotten Veterans and they are right, the big difference was the hostility shown the Vietnam Veterans by a sizable portion of the population. One only has to remember the movies that were made by Hollywood that depicted the Vietnam Veteran as a drudged crazed, psychopath. I'm talking about movies such as Born of the 4th of July, Deer Hunter, Apocalypse Now and others. After the dedication of the Vietnam Veterans Memorial on November 13, 1982, the American People began to separate the unpopular war from the ones who fought it. More than 8.7 million Americans served in Vietnam. There were 58, 151 deaths and 153, 303 who were wounded and 2,646 listed as unaccounted for.

The Vietnam Veterans Leadership Program that President Reagan put into every state was very instrumental in changing the public's attitude of the men and women who fought in that war. One notable outcome was the dedication and determination of Vietnam Veterans and all other Veterans to make sure the men and women who served in the War on Terrorism did not leave and come home to a hostile or indifferent reception. The Veterans worked very hard to make sure that these brave young volunteers knew that we loved them and supported them and their families. Huge crowds would come together in cities all across America, large and small to bid them farewell and to welcome them when they completed their tours.

Because the National Guard and Reserve units made up a large percentage of our forces, they would leave as a unit. In Jonesboro, Arkansas an Engineer Battalion, some 500 strong left as a unit for Fort McCoy, Wisconsin, for training, then on to Iraq. When they departed hundreds of citizens with flags and signs sent them on their way. They were at Fort McCoy during the Christmas holidays, the military could not fund the transportation cost of bringing them home for Christmas and New Years. The citizens of this area raised over $60,000.00 to rent buses to bring them home. Money was left over and was used to establish a Family Support Group that provided assistance to family members who had financial difficulties or simply needed assistance in work around the home. A small detachment from Vermont became part of the Battalion, they did not have the means to go back to Vermont, when the folks here found out about the situation, they paid for their transportation also.

The 875th Engineer Battalion, commanded by a female Lt. Col. with 500 members did a magnificent job in Iraq, their main job was to clear the road-side bombs, IEDs from the supply routes. They lost one member of the Battalion, with several wounded. When they returned home, people lined the main street leading into the Armory for miles, again with flags and welcome home signs.

This happened all across America, these fine young men and women are the best that America has to offer and we owe them so much for their service and sacrifices.

My only purpose in arranging the flight to Washington DC for the dedication ceremonies was to get as many Vietnam Veterans there in order to pay tribute to those who paid the ultimate sacrifice. My life was changed forever and led me to dedicated the rest of my life to helping those who have stepped forward in defense of our great country. I have met and worked with thousands of people since the dedication ceremonies, while I cannot list them all, I would like to share with you my most exciting times over the past twenty-seven years.

John Wayne (second from left) and Ron Miller (third from left).

November 19, 1982

Vietnam Special Flight, Inc.
825 Fairfield Drive
Marietta, GA 30067

Mr. Dave C. Garrett
President
Delta Air Lines, Inc.
Hartsfield Atlanta International Airport
Atlanta, GA 30320

Dear Mr. Garrett:

The L-1011 charter to Washington, D.C., on November 13, to attend the
dedication ceremonies of the Vietnam Memorial, was a complete success.
Our goals for the flight were to get as many veterans to Washington for
the least amount of money and to make the public aware of the five day
national tribute to Vietnam veterans.

Our success was due largely to the enthusiastic support of Delta Air
Lines. I would particularly like to thank Mr. Paul Huckfeldt and Jim
Hefferman for their assistance in obtaining the charter and expediting
the request to the Civil Aeronautics Board.

As you know the flight crew, Mr. Paul Smith, Pete Peterson, Ken Adams,
and the following flight attendants voluntered to fly the charter on
their day off.

Beverly Dubois	Helen Thompson
Kerry Ramsburger	Marlene Boddie
Paulette Massey	Linda Tinsley
Joanne Joiner	Martina Goshe
Susan Lee	Gillian Thomas
Susan Powell	

I have always known that Delta Air Lines was a great place to work,
and the generosity shown to us by the crew is just how fortunate we are
to have Delta here in Atlanta.

No one will ever know how valuable that trip was to the Vietnam
veterans. I received a phone call the following day from a former
enlisted man, who made the trip and his comment was, "I never felt like
I came home from Vietnam until we landed in Atlanta Saturday evening."
That comment was reward enough for me, and I would like to thank Delta
Air Lines for making it possible.

Thank you,

Ron Miller
Vietnam Veteran

RM/kn

DELTA AIR LINES, INC.

HARTSFIELD ATLANTA INTERNATIONAL AIRPORT

ATLANTA, GEORGIA 30320

DAVID C. GARRETT, JR.
PRESIDENT

November 30, 1982

Mr. Ron Miller
Vietnam Special Flight, Inc.
825 Fairfield Drive
Marietta, Georgia 30067

Dear Mr. Miller:

Thank you for your very nice letter recognizing our crew on
Flight 8202 of November 13 and also Paul Huckfeldt and Jim
Heffernan for their expeditious handling of the charter
arrangements.

Your wonderful commendation will be passed on to the individuals
you mentioned with my sincere thanks, too, for their exemplary
part in this special event. We are very proud of their performance. I am sure it was also a memorable experience for them
and that they will be most grateful for your generous comments.

We also appreciate your very positive evaluation of Delta and
it was very thoughtful of you to take the time to share your
feelings with us. We are keenly aware that Delta's success
depends on our ability to please our customers and it is
gratifying to know that our folks made such a favorable
impression. We consider our people to be our greatest asset.

Again, many thanks for your very considerate letter and we look
forward with pleasure to serving you in the future.

Sincerely,

David C Garrett

DCGjr:nmt

Av Westin
Vice President
Executive Producer

February 21, 1985

Mr. Ron Miller
Executive Director
Georgia
Vietnam Veterans Leadership Program
500 Northridge Road, N.E.
Suite 610
Atlanta, Georgia 30338

Dear Mr. Miller:

Your letter to Fred Pierce has been referred to me.

ABC News has devoted considerable coverage to the
importance of the Vietnam Memorial in bringing all
Americans together again.

Your incredible effort, chartering a plane to
bring 300 veterans to Washington may deserve some
further attention. We will consider it for 20/20
and if we decide to go ahead, we will be in touch.

Sincerely,

Av Westin
Vice President
Abc News

AW:bjh

The East Room in the White House.

VIETNAM SPECIAL FLIGHT, INC.

Chapter 2

President Ronald Reagan

AS I mentioned earlier in the book, Tom Pauken of Dallas, Texas was appointed the Director of ACTION, the all volunteer agency by President Reagan. The Vietnam Veterans Leadership Program was his idea and he convinced The President and Congress to make the funds available, which they did. True to President Reagan's philosophy of smaller Government, he agreed to fund it for 4 years, if the programs made a difference in their State , then funding would have to come from the private sector or state funds. The Georgia program, along with a handful of others, are still operating. I had three personal encounters with President Reagan and can remember them as if they happened yesterday. He came to Atlanta for a political event and I made sure I was there. I was working on a Bob Hope special in Atlanta. I took a brochure with me with the President's photo on the front. When Reagan finished he came into the crowd to shake hands. I positioned myself where I thought he would walk by, he did and I asked him for his autograph, while he signed it, I told him about the Hope Special and asked him if I could get a telegram to read at the event. He said sure, contact the White House and let them know we talked. I got the telegram.

Later, the President invited all the Directors of the Leadership Programs to the White House for a special event honoring Vietnam Veterans. I was lucky enough to be selected to be on the stage with him and met him again. I personally met him once more, he came to Columbus, Georgia to speak at a campaign event, while there, he signed the Veterans Administration Ominous bill, I was asked to assist in the activities, basically getting the Veteran leadership together, I was also asked to submit information about Veteran Issues, which I sent to the White House. After the signing event we walked to the Columbus Coliseum for the speech. I was standing in the audience, the President began his speech, about half way through I heard a couple sentences of my information that I sent to the White House, to this day I have not mentioned this, don't know why just have not.

The only other time I had contact with the White House and President Reagan was to ask for and receive a taped message from him that was played over the Stadium screen at a Atlanta Braves baseball game. He thanked the Braves for dedicating the game to Vietnam Veterans and encouraged the business community to get involved with the GVVLP. He was and will always remain my hero, he basically had to rebuild the Defense Department from the lack of support from President Carter and did something the Veterans had wished for decades, he elevated the Veterans Administration from an Agency to Secretary level and gave us a Cabinet seat at the table.

It was a sad day indeed when he passed away. I called my local newspaper, told the editor of my work with him, they sent a reporter out and talked with me for some time. The next day my story was on front page with photographs, the reporter captured my recollections and passion for President Reagan, the front page is framed and on my wall in a honored place.

We will never see the likes of President Reagan again. I sent the telegram (see insert) that President Reagan sent to be read at the Bob Hope special event on June 10, 1986 at the Fox Theater in Atlanta to the Reagan Library in California. I'm told it is displayed, one of these days I will make the trip to pay homage to a great President. President Reagan is famously known for his quotes, as a retired military officer, here are my two favorites. "Here's my strategy on the Cold War: We Win, they Lose," which is exactly what happened. The other quote, "Of the four wars in my lifetime none came about because the U.S. was too strong."

To Ron Miller
With best wishes, Nancy Reagan Ronald Reagan

EASYLINK MBX 2676144A001 10JUN86 13:13/16:18 EST
VIA: 882236
      WU INFOMASTER   1-008852A161 06/10/86
TO: 62582450

MAIL SAFE UD

WU INFOMASTER   1-008852A161 06/10/86
ICS IPMACAA ATL
ZCZC 00511 ATLANTA GA 06-10 0155P EST ACAA
TLX 882236 MAILSAFE UD
BT

ACA089(1247)(1-008418I161)PD 06/10/86 1242
TWX WHITEHOUSE WSH DLY PD
090 GOVT DLY WHITE HOUSE DC JUN 10
PMS MR RON MILLER EXECUTIVE DIRECTOR (DLR DONT DWR)
GEORGIA VIETNAM VETERANS LEADERSHIP PROGRAM
500 NORTHRIDGE ROAD NE SUITE 610
ATLANTA GA 30338

I AM PLEASED TO EXTEND WARM GREETINGS TO THE
MEMBERS OF THE GEORGIA VIETNAM VETERANS LEADERSHIP
PROGRAM AND TO ALL THOSE GATHERED TO HONOR A TRULY
GREAT AMERICAN, MR. BOB HOPE.

FOR OVER 4 DECADES BOB HAS BROUGHT HAPPINESS
AND JOY TO MILLIONS OF AMERICANS IN AND OUT OF UNIFORM
SERVING IN FOREIGN LANDS, SEPARATED FROM THEIR LOVED
ONES, AND OFTEN IN DANGER. FOR THESE MEN AND WOMEN,
CHRISTMAS WAS OFTEN MADE A LITTLE BRIGHTER BY THIS
GREAT-HEARTED AMERICAN WHOSE WIT IS EXCEEDED ONLY BY
HIS PATRIOTISM.
ALL AMERICAN OWE BOB HOPE A DEBT OF GRATITUDE
WE CAN NEVER REPAY. NANCY JOINS ME IN SENDING OUR
CONGRATULATIONS, OUR APPRECIATION, AND OUR FONDEST
GOOD WISHES TO BOB HOPE.
GOD BLESS YOU ALL.
RONALD REAGAN
NNNN

NNNN
1313 EST

MAIL SAFE UD

MMMM

VIETNAM SPECIAL FLIGHT, INC.

Chapter 3

President George H.W. Bush

IN 1979, I was in the last year of my career as a helicopter and mul-ti-engine airplane pilot and stationed at Fort Sam Houston, located in downtown San Antonio. I had a blast in San Antonio and al-most stayed there after I retired in August 1980. The Presidential elec-tion was under way and President Reagan and President Bush (41) op-posed each other in the Republican Primary. I decided to vote for Pres-ident Bush because of his vast experience, he was the former Director of the CIA and Ambassador to China, among many other high posi-tions. I knew nothing about President Reagan, other than he was the former Governor of California. Things worked out perfectly, Reagan served two great terms and Bush served eight years as Vice President and one term as President.

As I mentioned earlier, the Reagan Administration was a very strong supporter of the Military and Veterans; so when President Bush (41) became President, I continued to work, as much as I could for President Bush. I served as Georgia State Director, Veterans for Reagan/Bush in 1984 and Bush/Quayle in 1988 and 1992. I met VP Quayle and accompanied him on a campaign stop just south of Atlan-ta. He was a very likable man, very friendly and did a very good job on the campaign trail.

During a campaign stop in Atlanta, I was invited to meet President Bush (41) at plane side at Dobbins AFB in Marietta, Ga. because I had worked on the campaigns. Being a Veteran himself and a pilot, we had a very pleasant conversation, although brief he was very cordial and he knew of the work I had done for the campaign and knew about the Georgia Vietnam Veterans Leadership Program. President Bush was one of the youngest Naval Aviators during World War II, he flew a fighter/bomber and was shot down in the Pacific, he managed to para-chute into the Pacific and was extremely lucky that day. A submarine was in the area, surfaced and plucked him from the ocean, had it not been there, he would surely have died or captured by the Japanese and in all probability would have been killed.

Sometime later he awarded the GVVLP his Point of Light Award for community service. Myself and the Chairman of the Board, Mr.

Tommy Clack were invited to welcome President Bush on another trip to Atlanta. The President arrived at Dobbins AFB aboard the new Air Force One, a Boeing 747, it was beautiful. By that time I had observed that the President usually moved quickly down the receiving line and almost always spends more time with the last person in the line before departing.

I told Tommy this, we positioned ourselves at the end of the line, the President came down the steps of the aircraft and made his way down the line. The President was briefed on the people that he would meet. I was the Executive Director, full time paid employee and an appointee of the Reagan and now Bush Administration, Tommy was also a combat Vietnam Veteran, and a very well known Veteran in Georgia. Tommy was in a wheelchair, he had lost both legs and one arm at the shoulder during a mortar attack in Vietnam. It did not slow him down at all, as a matter of fact, he could outwork most people.

The President spent a considerable time with us, after all we three were combat Veterans. He said goodbye and got into the Limo and departed for downtown Atlanta for a speech. We had been told that we would be given a tour of Air Force One after the President departed. We were excited about the tour, Tommy looked at the ramp stairs that led to the door of the plane, the stairs were steep and very high. Tommy would have to be carried, in his wheel chair up the stairs, he said, let's go, I do not want to put the crew out. We started to make our way to the terminal and to our cars, about half-way to the terminal, we heard a Secret Service Agent call out for us to stop. He walked up and said, "President Bush called back to the airplane from the Limo and told the crew to make sure those two Veterans get the VIP tour of Air Force One." Tommy, again said we do not want to cause you any additional work, the agent replied, "We have our orders from the President.," and escorted us back to the stairs. It took four agents to get Tommy up the stairs and into the plane. All the other visitors turned right upon entering the plane, they took us to the left and showed us the President's personal quarters, the cockpit, the small operating room, we were told a surgeon was always on board the aircraft. We did indeed get the VIP treatment and they loaded us up with mementos from the tour, all kinds of gifts with the President's seal and logo of Air Force One, which I still display proudly in my home.

President Bush (41) was, in my humble opinion the nicest, most unassuming President that I have met or observed. It was very hard for me to understand how Bill Clinton, from my home state of Arkansas could beat him in the 92 election. As with Obama, the media had made it their mission to get Bill elected. It is all history now and I will not go into it; however I will share with you one of the reasons that President Bush (41) lost the support of a segment of the population that should never had happened, the Veteran vote.

President Bush appointed an individual as Secretary of the Veterans Affairs who thought he was doing the right thing by floating the idea that the VA could also treat Civilians at VA hospitals, if those hospitals were under-utilized. As you might expect, the Veteran Community was irate at this suggestion and some made it their mission to defeat President Bush. Some of the prominent Veteran leaders joined with Bill Clinton and when the dust settled, Clinton captured a majority of the Veteran votes. It was enough to ensure defeat for a very good President, one that should never had happened.

The campaign staff for the President was told time and time again that he should fire the VA Secretary, the President was loyal to a fault for sticking with him, I had a conversation and exchanged notes with Mary Matalin about the situation. The drive-by media was in the tank for Clinton and we could see a possible defeat. She understood and said the situation was not good.

I had teamed up with USMC General Ray Davis (Ret) a few years before to work on political efforts at the National and State level (see next chapter on General Davis). General Davis, who retired as Assistant Commandant, of the Marine Corps fought in three wars, WWII, Korea and Vietnam, he received the Medal of Honor for action at the Chosin Reservoir in Korea. We were told the President would visit Atlanta in a couple weeks on a campaign stop. I informed the State Republican Party of Georgia that General Davis and I could gather a large number of the Veteran Leadership from throughout the State at a venue in Atlanta, it would be the perfect opportunity to talk to these leaders and assure them that he was a strong supporter of Veterans issues and would never do anything to undermine the mission of the VA, which is to care for those who have served our Country.

The White House agreed, we got to work and assembled a very large number of Vets for the meeting, which was held at a new American Legion Post in a nearby suburb of Atlanta, Georgia, about 25 miles from the Hotel where the President was speaking.

General Davis and I arrived early, were escorted to a hallway behind the large room where the President was speaking. At the end of the speech, we saw several Secret Service Agents heading our way, followed by the President and some of his staff. He greeted Gen. Davis and myself and spoke briefly, then we began moving down the hall and outside where the Limo and several support vehicles were lined up. As we approached the Limo, General Davis and I prepared to move to a vehicle behind the Limo, the President said, "You gentlemen are riding with me," I was shocked and very surprised.

General Davis sat in a jump seat facing the Chief of Staff, Mr. Skinner and I sat directly opposite President Bush, somehow I managed to keep my composure, if we had known about this before hand, I probably could not have done it.

On the way to the event, we briefed the President on the problems with the Veteran vote, while we did not recommend that he fire the VA Secretary, we told him of the situation and he appeared to understand and accept it.

Somehow the topic of Jane Fonda came up, the President shared with us a situation that came up with him a short time before. I have never heard this story before or since and with time passage, I'm sure President Bush would not mind me talking about it.

Queen Elisabeth of Great Britain invited President Bush to attend a huge celebration. While I cannot be certain of the exact title, I believe it was her Silver Jubilee Celebration, 50 years of serving as Queen. A short time later President Bush was informed that Jane Fonda was also invited. The President instructed his staff to let them know that he would not attend if she were in attendance. Ms. Fonda was disinvited. My respect for the President could not have gone any higher. The readers will also see another run-in with Ms Fonda with a meeting with Secretary of Defense Dick Cheney in Atlanta and another event described later on.

General Davis and I spent 50 minutes riding in the Limousine with the President and his Chief of Staff, hence the original name of this book.

Toward the end of the campaign the pressure would build from the Veteran Community, President Bush did fire the VA Secretary, it was too late and sadly we could not recover.

Sadly to say the polls indicated the President lost a majority of the Veteran vote and the election, an event that sadden me to no end and unfortunately gave us a President who abused the trust of the American people and also started us down the path that we find ourselves in today. Had it not been for a Republican House and Senate, we would have suffered a great deal more. Enough said about that.

I met the President a couple more times, once at the huge event that Disney put on at Disney World; celebrating all the Nation's Point

of Light recipients. A grand celebratio
CEO of Disney World.

I have also had the honor of being
dent Bush on numerous occasions, th
Photo taken with an athlete that wen'
Arkansas State University. I sent hirr
athlete and him, he responded quickly

Lastly, not too long after we start(
he reached in his coat pocket and saic
form!" and handed us a gold tie clip wiтн тне _
ple days later, we received a beautiful short note thanking us ioi ...
trip. Both are hanging on my wall. I will always remember him as a
very good President, a Gentleman and for my part, a great friend.

I am a financial supporter of the George H. W. Bush Presidential
Library Foundation located at Texas A&M University and I received
the 2010 calendar. He has a quote for each month, this is the one for
December, " Character matters....After all, you can't take it with you
as the saying goes, and when your time on earth is done and your
bones return to dust, no one will recall what kind of car you drove or
what kind of suit you had on... They'll remember if you kept your
word and played by the rules and loved your family." President
George H. W. Bush.

To Ron Miller with best wishes, G. Bush

THE PRESIDENT

March 2, 1992

Dear Ron:

Thanks for being with me when we went to the American Legion Hall on Saturday. I loved the event, and I loved visiting with the leaders of the Veteran groups from all across Georgia. How great of you to set it up.

Barbara joins me in sending warmest best wishes.

Sincerely,

G. Bush

VIETNAM SPECIAL FLIGHT, INC.

President Bush's limousine in front of the White House.

Chapter 4

Senator Bob Dole

I have been a big admirer of Senator Bob Dole from Kansas for many years. Three of my older brothers, Ralph, Bill and Owen served during WWII. One landed at Normandy and was seriously wounded. Sometime later, the other two were disabled to some extent. Senator Dole was an officer in the Army and leading his troops up a hill in Italy when he was badly wounded. He lay on the battlefield for eight hours before he was taken to a medical unit.

Standard Operating Procedures dictated that no one stopped the assault to care for a wounded comrade. Had that happened, it would take too much time and jeopardize the attack. One of his Sergeants saw Dole hit and ran to him to patch him up as best as possible and give him morphine. In all probability, it saved his life.

Senator Dole made the decision to run for President against President Clinton. He won the primary and picked Mr. Kemp as his running mate. My plan was to work the Georgia Veterans for the Senator as I had done before. A couple of friends who were lawyers in D.C. asked me to send them my National Veterans outreach plan and asked me if I would be interested in applying for the job with Senator Dole. The lawyers were Adrian Cronauer and Tom Burch. You may recognize Cronauer's name, he wrote the book, "Good Morning Vietnam," his story as a USAF disk jockey in Vietnam. Adrian sold the rights to the story to Hollywood and Robin Williams played Adrian in the movie. Adrian was one helluva comedian. I will share a funny story about Adrian a little later.

I sent them the plan. They talked to the folks in the Dole Campaign and invited me to D.C. to discuss the possibilities of running the National Veterans for Dole/Kemp. There I met Tom Carter, a former Air Force Pilot and a pilot for U.S. Airways. Tom was well known in the Military community and on Capitol Hill. His most high profile job in the military was to be a military aide to President Reagan, he carried the infamous football for the President. He was physically close to the President at all times , because he carried the necessary codes to initiate a nuclear war, if the need should arise.

I briefed the campaign staff on my plan and reviewed my involvement in campaigns going back several years. A couple days later, Tom Carter called and asked me if I belong to any Veteran Organizations. I informed him that I was a life member of several of the biggest organizations such as The Veterans of Foreign Wars, The American Legion and several more. A few days later, Tom called and said I had the job. He told me when to report for duty.

I put my great party home on the market, sold all my furniture, put my other belongings in storage, resigned my position as Executive Director of the Georgia Veterans Leadership Program (we had change the name because we now provided assistance to all Veterans, not just Vietnam Veterans) after thirteen years of some of the most enjoyable work that I had ever been involved with. It was with some sadness that I gave it up, but I left it in good hands. Tony Hamilton had run the Employment and Training Office for the entire time, and I knew he could do a great job. Andy Farris still ran the small business program and most of the original members of the Board of Directors were still in place.

As I mentioned before, I convinced the campaign and especially Senator Dole to name General Ray Davis, USMC (Ret) the National Chairman, Veterans for Dole/Kemp. I learned a very valuable lesson with the GVVLP, hook your star to smart, talented and true professionals and you will succeed.

After a few days in D.C., I found that I needed to round out the office with additional Veterans that would assist me in the enormous task of organizing all 50 states, Puerto Rico and The Virgin Islands. Soon Colonel Wil Ebel was running the effort with the National Guard and Reserves and Erwin "Swede" Huelsewede, USAF retired Chief Master Sergeant worked with me in organizing the states. Both were extremely competent and made my job much easier. We also had volunteers that would work in the office on a regular basis.

As a career Army Officer, I noticed right away that we had a serious problem at the head of the campaign staff. Senator Dole had given two campaign operatives Co-Chairman responsibilities, in other words, we did not have one boss that made the final decision. It became obvious that this would not work, even to Senator Dole. He let one go, I was somewhat disappointed because he was the one that I really wanted to work with. This individual would later become the Campaign Chairman for Senator Thompson's run for the Presidency.

Ask anyone who has ever worked in a National campaign, or for that matter at the State level and they will tell you to get ready for combat. Everyone seemed to be jockeying for the ear of the candidate, always trying to make a name for themselves within the system. It can lead to some very trying times within the office and on the campaign trail.

A couple of examples, we had one political director, the crew in the Vets office referred to him as Incabod Crane. He was constantly giving the volunteer staff a hard time, most of the time it was the women or young interns. One day he stuck his head in my office and made a wise remark about something that I had done in Florida. He left to go to his office. I followed him in, shut the door and told him, if he ever said something like that to me again, I would kick his ass up and down the hall for all to see, he could see I was serious and others in the vicinity overheard me. Bullies have always got my goat and I unloaded on him to no end.

Someone told Colonel Carter, he asked me to go down to the cafeteria located in the D.C. CNN Center adjacent to our headquarters. He asked me what had happened, I told him, about that time the object of my tirade walked by, he called him over and asked us to patch things up, we both did and I never had another problem with him.

At some point, it was obvious that Senator Dole could not be the Majority Leader in the Senate and run for President full-time. He did the courageous thing, something most would not do. He resigned from the Leader's position. We attended the news conference, he became a little emotional, but it was the right thing to do. The campaign needed a strong voice and leader, for some reason the Senator left the operation up to the staff, we had hoped he would kick a little fanny, it was not his style.

A very funny thing happened with Adrian Cronauer, Adrian was a great speaker, the Veteran community always turned out for his visits across the nation. Not only was he very funny, but he knew the issues that were important to Veterans. One day he was in the west somewhere speaking to a veterans group, Mrs. Dole was also there and a network film crew was following her around making a story about the "day in the life of the candidate's wife"

Adrian told this joke, "President Clinton returned to DC from an overseas trip, he was transported from Andrews AFB by Marine one, the Presidential helicopter. When Clinton left the helicopter at the White House, he was carrying a small white poodle dog that was given to him in Paris. The Marine Sergeant standing at the bottom of the helicopter steps said, 'Sir, nice dog Sir!' The President said, 'Yes! I got this for Hillary'. The Marine Sgt. said, 'Sir, nice swap Sir'. Well as you might expect, the film crew asked Mrs. Dole what she thought about the joke. She responded, that's just Adrian making jokes. Sometime later someone from the campaign manager's office called me and told me to tell Adrian not to tell that joke again. To my knowledge he did not, at least I never heard about it.

The drive-by media made it their mission to paint Senator Dole as a dark humorless candidate, when in reality; he had and still has a remarkable sense of humor. He could not get a break from the Press, they stayed on him constantly, always looking for the negative.

Our tiny staff was able to organize a very active Veterans program in every State, Puerto Rico and the Virgin Islands. Even the media reported that we had a very viable program by any standards. Polls after the election did indeed say we captured a sizable majority of the Veteran vote. Alas, it was not enough and we lost, we gave the good fight, it was just not enough.

There are countless other stories that I could tell about the campaign, Mrs. Dole was a delight to work for, she was very friendly and always made us feel welcome, was not the case for some of the other staff. Why, no one knows.

One day the campaign Director, the one that was let go called me into his office and said Congress was studying a bill that would determine if the Veteran's preference was to remain for Veterans applying for a job with the Federal Government. The current law gave the Veteran a 5 or 10 point advantage in hiring over non-vets. Some women groups objected because they felt that it discriminated against women. What they did not take into consideration was that women made up about 14 percent of the military and could also take advantage of the law. The political director of the campaign, a woman was dead set against the preference. The Director called us both in, we made our argument and he sided with me and Senator Dole voted that way. He told us both that he would always come down on the side of service to our country in determining his decision.

One of the most memorable events that I work on involved Air Force Generals Tibbets and Sweeney, pilots of the Enola Gay and Bock's Car, the two B-29s that dropped Atomic Bombs on Hiroshima and Nagasaki, Japan during World War II. I was out west. I cannot remember the city, representing Senator Dole at the annual convention of one of the major Veteran Service Organizations.

The crews of the two B-29s were there as special guests and were signing autographs for the assembled Veterans. I had the opportunity to meet both crews and I asked them to please call me if they came to D.C., and I would set up a meeting with Senator

A couple weeks later, General Tibbets called and said they had been invited to a meeting in the Capital. I arranged for a meeting with the Senator, went by their Hotel and picked up both crews in a medium size tour bus.

The wives of both Generals had passed away and they had married younger, very attractive ladies. The crews sat together on either side of the bus and you could hear the good natured talks between the crews, General Tibbets and the crew of the Enola Gay had received the bulk of the press over the years because they dropped the first Atomic bomb. It was indeed interesting to hear their discussions.

We arrived at Senator Dole's office; the crews were complete, except the Co-Pilot of the Enola Gay had passed away some time earlier. They had a long excellent visit, and they made several pictures with Senator Dole and the entire crew.

My brother, Owen had served in the Navy and was stationed on Tinian Island where the B-29s were stationed. He met some of the crew of the Enola Gay, especially the crew chief, once he allowed my brother to tour the inside of the plane, of course no one there knew about the mission.

My brother was elected as a State Representative in The Arkansas House and served twelve years. He invited General Tibbets and his crew to visit the State Capital and gave them the VIP tour. The newspapers wrote a very nice article about the visit. I met General Tibbets once more in Roswell, Georgia some time after that.

One thing I will always remember about General Tibbets, a newspaper reporter asked him once if he ever regretted dropping the Atomic Bomb on Japan. His comment was, "I never lost a minute sleep over my actions." It was estimated that hundreds of thousands of Americans would have died if we had invaded Japan.

I met Ron Ray a former Assistant Secretary of the VA and a Medal of Honor recipient from Vietnam during the campaign. He had worked as a consultant in Romania and when the campaign was winding down, he asked me if I would be interested in working for a month in Bucharest with some of the members of their Conservative Parties. The were attempting to write a plan that would consolidate several parties into one, as they had never had a democratic election.

I was to be paid my expenses and $5000.00 for my efforts. Luckily I had met Tony Blankley's wife, who was a consultant for the Dole campaign. She informed me that Tony had worked in Romania and I asked her to set up a meeting with him. I met Tony and he gave me an excellent overview of the Romanian Government and some of the problems he encountered.

I also met with the Republican National Committee in DC and was provided the organizational plan for the RNC. It was very helpful, I probably could not have accomplished such an enormous undertaking without their plan, which included the Standard Operating Procedures of the organization.

I was housed at a very nice villa owned by the doubles partner of Nastasia, their Tennis National Hero. I really enjoyed my time there, spent a great deal of time working, but had some time to enjoy the nightlife.

I was invited to attend their remarkable celebration in the main square of Bucharest on the night of the first free election in Romania's history, the results came in at 4 PM with hundreds of thousands of people in the square when the announcement that the first freely elected President in their history was announced over the loud speakers. At once, the people dropped to their knees and a Priest, who had been imprisoned under the former dictator said the Lord's Prayer. It was a very emotional event. Most all the Romanians were in tears.

At the end of the ceremony a young Romanian man walked up and introduced himself to me, said he had walked 30 miles to be at the ceremony. He told me that he had visited the United States as an exchange student, made possible by his Church. I asked him where he lived while in the U.S. I nearly fainted when he said my hometown of Jonesboro, Arkansas. He also gave me a flag that the new President had signed for him, I told him that he should keep it, he was adamant and I finally accepted it. I gave him some money and told him to take a taxi home.

In the early part of 1996, I went to California to represent Senator Dole at the American Veterans Chamber of Commerce. It was quite a treat. Adrian Cronauer was there in typical form, along with a host of retired Generals and Admirals. I had a chance to meet and talk with General Westmoreland, Vice Admiral James B. Stockdale, Admiral U.S.G. Sharp, all retired from their respective services.

Over a dozen actors and actresses were there, and I had the great pleasure of sitting next to Connie Stevens, she was a great star in motion pictures, television, Broadway, recording and in concerts. She performed overseas for the military in Vietnam and the Persian Gulf. The others included, James Avery, who starred in "The Fresh Prince of Bel Air," Joe Conley, "The Waltons," Troy Evans of the TV series "China

Beach" and a combat Vietnam Veteran, Ron Harper who starred in many prime time series, Tony LoBianco, a Tony Award nominee and Emmy Winner, Joseph Mascolo, of the soap opera, "Days of Our Lives," Robert Pine, star of "CHIPs," Bruce Sievers, a super poet, who was a Green Beret in Vietnam, and Mamie Van Doren, one of the three M's, Marilyn, Mansfield and Mamie, she starred in over 50 movies and performed for three months in Vietnam with her one-woman variety show.

One of my favorites that evening was Mr. Les Brown and His Band of Renown, who served as the Music Director for Bob Hope on 18 overseas Christmas shows and three around-the-world tours. He was a very friendly man and I talked to him at length about my relationship with Mr. Hope.

Working at the Dole campaign was quite an experience, one that I will never forget. I met some very important people, General Colin Powell, many U.S. Senators and Congressmen, one that I really like was Senator Alan Simpson from Wyoming. He was truly a delight and my kind of man. Several years later I stopped in at the famous Western Museum in Cody, Wyoming. They had a very nice store in the museum that sold all kinds of things, including the Senator' new book, "Right In The Old Gazoo." I told the lady there that I had worked for Senator Dole and had met Senator Simpson a couple of times. She told me that he had an office in the museum, but that he was on the road giving a speech. She said leave the book, give me your mailing address and I will ask him to sign it. Several days later I received the book and Senator Simpson said he did indeed remember me and wrote a full page of remarks, it is proudly displayed in my home.

To Ron:
Thanks for all your hard work: *Bob* and *Elizabeth*

VIETNAM SPECIAL FLIGHT, INC.

Chapter 5

General Raymond G. Davis
Medal of Honor, USMC (Ret)

O F all the people I have met since the flight, General Davis is unequalled and the man I most admired. He was born on January 13, 1915, in Fitzgerald, Georgia, and a graduate from Georgia Tech, where he made the honor roll each year. He was a member of the Army Reserve Officer Training Corp (AROTC). They had a Navy ROTC program there and he made the decision to join the United States Marine Corps with a regular commission.

The difference in my eyes from General Davis and other General Officers that I have met is that he led by example. To quote Marine General Carl Hoffman, "He was never a shouter, never profane, never a grandstander. Ray Davis expressed his thoughts with gentlemanly precision and razor-sharp logic, never closed his mind on a topic, ever remaining willing to reopen the dialogue or reconsider a decision. His soft-spoken guidance carried more authority than the strident bellowing of some other leaders." He was quite, but no one ever took that as weakness. He was a strong willed man who could get the job done and was simply a genius in my eyes.

General Creighton W. Abrams, Jr., who commanded the U.S. Military Assistance Command in Vietnam from 1968-1972, once observed during the Commandant of Marine Corps visit to Vietnam he said, "Of the fifty or so Division Commanders I have known in Vietnam, General Davis has no peer. He's the best!" General Davis was the Assistant Commandant of the Marine Corps when he retired, most everyone assumed he would be the Commandant, but fate had a hand to play.

The Pentagon was recommending General Davis to be the Commandant. General Davis was not sure he would get it, because of the personal relationship between President Nixon and General Cushman. General Cushman was assigned earlier as Vice President Nixon's military aide and may have save Nixon's life by pushing Nixon to the floor of the Presidential limousine and shielding him from radical demonstrators during a trip to South America. In the end, President Nixon appointed Cushman as Commandant and General Davis retired from his beloved Marine Corp. He returned to Georgia in 1972 where he was appointed Executive Vice President of the Chamber of Commerce for the State of Georgia. I met him at a political rally in the mid-80s and we worked in the political arena for over 20 years.

In 1987 General Davis joined with Army General Richard Stilwell to design and plan for the building of the Korean War Veterans memorial in Washington, D.C. Sometime later, General Stillwell died and General Davis, and others, completed and dedicated the Memorial.

During our ride in the Presidential Limo in 1992 with President George H.W. Bush, General Davis took the opportunity to let the President know that he had been trying to get the White House to schedule the President to attend the ground breaking ceremony for the Memorial and had not yet gotten a commitment. President Bush turned to the Chief of Staff and said, "Schedule it!"

As it happened, President Bush lost the election and President Clinton attended the dedication ceremony in 1995. We were not sure if President Clinton knew General Davis was the National Chairman for Veterans for Dole. What an ironic twist of fate? It was a great ceremony, our only regret was that President Bush was not there. I was there accompanying Senator Bob Dole who was running for President against President Clinton. I sat directly behind Senator Dole. There was one vacant seat two seats down from me. Senator John Glenn arrived and moved down to take that seat. I pecked Senator Dole on the arm and told him that Senator Glenn had arrived. He looked back and said, "What are you doing here? Why are you not up there?" pointing to the stage. Senator Glenn was a hero of the Korean War, where he flew fighters. Senator Glenn just shrugged and smiled. Later we found out that the White House staff had also failed to invite Senator Glenn to the reception at the White House after the ceremonies. The media brought it up. The White House sent over a quick invite and Senator Glenn attended. Being the gentleman he was, he never mentioned the slight.

One humorous thing happened as Senator Dole and I were leaving the event. A gentleman called out to the Senator, motioned him to come over and meet his friend, a Korean War Veteran that he brought to the ceremony. Dole walked over and shook their hand, made some small talk, then we departed. He asked me who was the young guy he had just met. It was Billy Ray Cyrus. His song, "Achy Break Heart," was a big hit at the time. Senator Dole had not heard of him. I was with the Senator because I had been selected as his Executive Director for Veterans for Dole and worked for him at the Campaign Headquarters in D.C. for almost two years, 1995-1996.

When I was selected, I put a full court press on at the campaign headquarters to name General Ray Davis as the National Chairman for Veterans for Dole. As soon as Dole got my memo, he sent a notice back to the headquarters to name the General quickly. I will elaborate more about this later. General Davis and I worked very hard on the Dole campaign. We rolled out the announcement of our team at the George State Capital in Atlanta. We had a great turn-out for the event. He and I traveled on behalf of the Senator. One of the most memorable events was the annual parade in Miami held by the Cuban community. General Davis wore his dress white Marine uniform. The reception among the people was unbelievable! He really enjoyed the event. Just so happened the Marine Band from D.C. was there and they had a special musical event for him.

Marine General Jones was the Commandant of the Marine Corps. He was also General Davis' Aide-de-Camp in Vietnam when the General commanded the 3rd Marine Division. General Jones dedicated the famed ceremony the Marine Barracks, 8th and I to General Davis. I was invited to attend, where I met General Jones and other Marine dignitaries, plus several Congressmen and Senators. It was a splendid ceremony, one that I thoroughly enjoyed and will always remembers.

I was visiting with a good friend, Alex Mason in Myrtle Beach, South Carolina. Alex was a combat Vietnam Veteran and served in the Air Force, flew with Eastern Airline until they went belly-up, and he started his own small business in the textile industry and did quite well. I received a phone call that General Davis had gone to the hospital and died of a heart attack while there. I immediately left for Atlanta. It was one of the saddest trips of my life. I admired General Davis. I respected him. He was one of the nicest men you would ever meet. He died on September 3, 2003, and was buried in a Veterans Cemetery just south of Atlanta.

Senator Zell Miller, Governor Perdue, The Commandant of the Marine Corps, General Hagee and hundreds of Marines, Medal of Honor recipients and thousands of other people attended his funeral. The burial site was miles away from the church services. The local police departments and the Georgia State Patrol conducted a rolling road block on the freeways, the exact same as accorded a Presidential visit.

It was a sad day for me and thousands of other people. We lost a great hero. When he passed away, he was the most highly decorated Veteran alive, not just Marine Corps, but of all the services. In addition to the Medal of Honor, he received the Navy Cross, two Distinguished Service Medals, two Silver Stars, two Legion of Merits, Bronze Start, Purple Heart and scores of service medals.

There will never be another General Davis. You can read his book, *The Story of Ray Davis.* You can also read more about his incredible Marine Corps service and his life on the internet.

This is one of my favorite quotes from him, "Above all, I see myself as a man of action. I never sit around and think about others doing this or that...I am aware that as a holder of the Medal of Honor, I belong to this nation forever because of a combat situation where literally thousands of men's lives depended on the actions that I took when someone had to take action." His Medal of Honor citation for his actions at the Chosin Reservoir in Korea can be found on the internet.

Ron Miller
3-2-92

Ray Davis
3-2-92
CMOH

Geo Bush
6-2-00

Chapter 6

Bob Hope

I N 1966, I was stationed at Chu Chi, Vietnam with the 116th Assault Helicopter Company. I flew the Huey Gunship equipped with six .30 cal. machine guns and 14 aerial rockets. The unit supported the famed 25th Infantry Division which had been stationed in Hawaii. We got the news that Bob Hope would be bringing his famous USO show to our area.

I was notified that I would be flying anti-mortar patrol at another show at Long Binh, one of the largest bases in the area. Several thousand troops would be in attendance and the Commanders were concerned the Viet Cong would attempt to launch mortars into the show site with the possibility of killing and wounding scores of troops and maybe evening killing some of the performers. Think of the world wide publicity if they could do that.

I took three gunships to the headquarters areas, and we provided constant cover until the show had completed and the performers had left the area. We knew the start time of the performance, and we arrived a little early to take aerial photos of thousands of troops that had gathered at the site.

Bob Hope definitely had a soft spot when it came to American Servicemen at war. For decades, Mr. Hope traveled around the globe with some of the top entertainers providing a break for the troops. Ask any man or woman who had the opportunity to see his show, and they will tell you it was the best thing that could have happened to them.

The USO was created in 1941 during World War II, they approached Mr. Hope in May to host a show at March Airfield in California. He was not too sure he wanted to do it, but agreed. He and the show were welcomed by, "...the best audience in the world." His last USO show overseas was in the Middle East during the War on Terrorism.

To thank Mr. Hope for his lasting dedication to our servicemen and women, the USO dedicated its world headquarters in Washington, D.C., to "America's Number 1 soldier in greasepaint." He has met all the Presidents since the 1940's, played golf with most of them, mingled with heads of states from around the world, but was most comfortable around the military.

In 1985, I was looking at some of my photo albums and discovered the photos of his show and began thinking about the possibilities of getting Mr. Hope to do a show for the Vietnam Veterans in Atlanta, Georgia. A few days later, as fate would have it, I read an article in the Atlanta papers that Bob Hope would be coming to Atlanta to perform at the famous Fox Theatre. I decided to write him a letter and ask him to consider putting on a special show for Vietnam Veterans. I have included the letter that I wrote to Mr. Hope and his response. Later Mr. Hope informed me that he had a contract with NBC and could not appear on another TV network. That was cancelled and we started discussing the possibility of him doing a special night for Veterans prior to his performance in Atlanta in June 1986. After some time, we managed to put all the pieces together and the show was scheduled for June 10, 1986.

I am very glad to have had the experience in putting together the flight to Washington, D.C. which required weeks of long days and nights to make the necessary arrangements to make it a success. While the Bob Hope Special was a daunting task, it did not compare to the hard work required to make the flight a reality.

For one thing, Bob Hope was an icon in the American conscience. He was a beloved actor, comedian and a true hero to Veterans and their families. For years, Mr. Hope was the only citizen to be named an "Honorary Veteran" by an act of Congress. A few years ago, Mr. Zack Fisher was also given the honor of being named an Honorary Veteran for building the numerous "Fisher Houses" near military hospitals for free lodging for families visiting their sons and daughters who were in treatment. I also had the honor of meeting Mr. Fisher at an event in honor of General William C. Westmoreland. I had a long conversation with him and thanked him for his dedication to Veterans and their families.

Mr. Hope was to appear at the beautiful Fox Theater in downtown Atlanta. We met with the manager of the Fox and they agreed to rent us the fabulous Egyptian Ballroom, where countless parties and events had been held for decades. It was a superb venue that would be perfect for the reception with Mr. Hope and the leaders of the community.

A great deal of cash would have to be raised to pay for the ballroom decorations, flowers, food, brochures, a gift for Mr. Hope and the miscellaneous expenses to make this a huge success. Our major sponsors were Texaco, MCI Telecommunications, Coors and the Coca-Cola Bottling Company, and others too numerous to list. One that gave me great satisfaction was Carithers Flowers in my hometown of Marietta, Georgia. I stopped in one day and spoke with the owner and told him about Mr. Hope's tribute to Vietnam Veterans. I also mentioned that I would give him free tickets to the event for him and his family. He said that would be fine, but he was willing to donate the flowers no matter. They delivered the fresh flowers in the afternoon. We were amazed at the number of separate flower arrangements. Mr. Carithers made the center arrangement that was over five feet high and was the most beautiful arrangement that I had ever seen.

The Atlanta Braves, Mr. Bob Larsen, the Military Task Force of the Atlanta Chamber of Commerce, The Gainesville Chamber, the Georgia Department of Veterans Services, Commissioner Pete Wheeler and many others assisted in outreaching the veteran community to announce the performance.

The big night arrived. Mr. Hope and his beautiful wife, Dolores, arrived early and spent over thirty minutes at the reception. Governor Joe Frank Harris, his wife and others greeted them at the reception. Andy Farris, the person responsible for establishing our extremely successful Small Business Program for Veterans, wanted to present our Small Business Awards at the reception. I told him it was a great idea and we presented seven awards to Veterans who excelled in the business arena.

The highlight of the reception was the performance by Marina Alden Bryant, President of World Events, Inc. Instead of trying to remember everything about the performance, I will include the entire letter she wrote to me at the passing of Mr. Hope in 2003. Her performance of "Thanks for the Memories," Mr. Hope's signature song was a masterpiece.

Mr. Hope's performance at the Fox was a smash success. He came on stage, had a huge orchestra, entertained us for over an hour, and without one single cue-card. His wife, Dolores, also sang a few songs. She was great!

Toward the end of the performance, Mr. Hope asked me to come on stage and before thousands of his fans. I read the telegram from President Reagan to Mr. Hope and those in attendance.

I did not have a hard copy of the telegram that evening. I gave Mr. Hope the copy and sent him a hard copy later. As Marina said in her 2003 letter, "Mr. Bob Hope lived his passion to live life to the fullest and to give laughter and entertain. He will be missed but never forgotten."

In February 2009, I visited Palm Springs, California. While there, a friend gave us a tour of the area. He showed us Mr. Hope's home on a hillside overlooking the city. He also informed us that Mr. Hope donated the beautiful large and very expensive home to the city after he passed away. They use it for special events.

I have made some mistakes in my life, some that I regret, but the biggest mistake occurred when Mr. Hope passed away. I was in Los Angeles with Alex Wells, Jr. and his wife, Mary Thibaudeau. We were meeting with ALCON Productions, which is owned by Fred Smith, Chairman and Chief Executive Officer of Federal Express, which I will tell you about later on in the book. I was invited to Mr. Hope's memorial service, but ALCON had scheduled some important meetings with the movers and shakers in the movie industry. They convinced me to attend those instead of the service. A monumental mistake on my part, and I deeply regret it to this day. I also talk about my involvement in the movie effort and Mr. Hope's offer to assist. You can read about them in the Perfume River chapter.

A few weeks later, Ann Margaret performed at the Fox Theater. I called a friend at the Fox and asked her to relay a message that I would be there and would like to meet her. After the show, I was escorted back stage. She traveled with Mr. Hope on the USO Tours. I showed her the picture of Mr. Hope and me that was taken at the Fox. She autographed it and thanked me for my service. She was with her husband, Roger Smith, who was a television star for several years.

Mr. Hope and I continued to correspond until 1991. I have a dozen personal letters from him and his great autograph on two posters, one was a large advertisement encouraging Americans to buy war bonds during World War II. He sign it, "To Ron: Thanks for the Memory, Bob Hope." He is my favorite entertainer of all time. No one comes close!

BOB HOPE

July 1, 1986

Mr. Ron Miller
Executive Director
Georgia VVLP, Inc.
500 Northridge Road, N.E.
Suite 610
Atlanta, GA   30338

Dear Ron:

That was a great night you did at the Fox in Atlanta, and I enjoyed it.

I'm sorry that I was in such a rush and couldn't attend the cocktail party a little more because they sure looked like beautiful people. I understand the Governor was awful happy...even though I didn't introduce him. I talked to him on the phone after that and he said "you didn't have to apologize to me, because I thought the night was a very inspirational night." I really enjoyed it. I'm sorry Westy didn't get there but I guess he was on his way to Chicago to do that affair there.

It was nice to see you and I'm going to give your script to a couple of important readers and see what they think about it.

Hope you are well.

Regards,

Bob

BH/lp

BOB HOPE

1986 OCT 10 PM 3: 37

October 3, 1986

Mr. Ron Miller
Director for Defense and
    Veterans Affairs
c/o The Honorable Mack Mattingly
United States Senator
Washington, D.C.   20510

Dear Ron:

Nice hearing from you and especially hearing
about the good news. I'm glad you have things
working.

Yes, I think I would be interested in a part
in that movie if it fit my character. I read
it and I thought it was very interesting.

I enjoyed doing the show in Atlanta and I'm
sorry I didn't have more time so I could really
have met all those fellows because they were a
great group. I meet them all over the country
and it brings back a lot of memories.

Hope you are enjoying great health and keep me
informed.

Regards,

Bob Hope

GEORGIA
Vietnam Veterans Leadership Program, Inc.

500 Northridge Road, N.E.
Suite 610
Atlanta, Georgia 30338
Ph: 404 998-7200

March 22, 1985

Mr. Bob Hope
10346 Moorpark Avenue
North Hollywood, CA 91602

Dear Mr. Hope:

I called Mr. Leo Thorsness, Chairman of the
Los Angeles Vietnam Veterans Leadership Program
and asked for your address.

The Georgia Vietnam Veterans Leadership Program has received a commitment from Mr. Ted Turner
to film a benefit special in Atlanta for Vietnam
veterans. Mr. Turner will show the one hour special
during prime time to the fifty states covered by
his cable system.

We respectfully ask that you consider joining
us as the Master of Ceremonies. We are currently
seeking a named entertainer and will have no difficulties in securing suitable entertainment;
however, we will accept any recommendations from
you on performers.

We have asked Coca-Cola, with its headquarters
here in Atlanta, to be the prime sponsor for the
television special and we have received a tentative
approval on March 22, 1985 (letter attached). Of
course, we will pay all expenses for you and the
entertainers you choose to bring with you. The
date of the special will be up to you, subject to
the availability of the Omni entertainment complex.

If you have any questions as to the film project, I can arrange for Mr. Turner or his Vice
President for Communications, Mr. Arthur Sando,
to give you or your representative a call.

We have an outstanding program here in Georgia
that is supported by the Governor, Max Cleland,
Secretary of State, corporations and the public. I
can assure you that you will receive an extremely
enthusiastic welcome from the people of Georgia and
the benefits will be nationwide for the Vietnam
veteran.

Mr. Bob Hope
March 22, 1985
Page Two

There are four people that I have greatly
admired and respected in my lifetime. My parents
who moved to Arkansas in the 1930's, cleared 40
acres of land, and raised eight children. My
father and four brothers served in the military.
Winston Churchill, who never lost faith. John
Wayne, whom I worked with for three months as a
helicopter safety consultant on "Green Berets",
and Bob Hope for your life long support and caring
for the men and women in uniform.

I thank you for your benevolence and consideration.

Respectfully,

Ron Miller
Executive Director
Georgia-VVLP

RM:ch
Enclosures

P.S. I was a helicopter gun ship pilot in
Vietnam during *1966.*   My responsibility
on two occasions was to provide continuous
air support against possible mortar attacks
for your shows at Long Binh and Cu-Chi.
I have included a photo of Long Binh during
your performance. Believe me, it was an
honor to do it and if you recall, not one
mortar round fell on your performance.

BOB HOPE

April 2, 1985

Ron Miller
Executive Director
Georgia Vietnam Veterans
  Leadership Program, Inc.
500 Northridge Rd., N.E., Ste. 610
Atlanta, Georgia 30338

Dear Ron Miller:

I read your letter and certainly enjoyed
that picture of Long Binh. Believe me, it
was an honor to do it, and if you recall,
not one mortar round fell on your performance.

That's a very interesting thing you're
talking about, having a one-hour special
for the Georgia Vietnam veterans. I'm in
favor of that and I hope we can work out
some kind of date. We can gather as many
of our people who went with us on those
trips and go back there and do that hour.
It would really be something.

Let me know what time schedule you have in
mind and we'll try and work it out.

                    Regards,

North Hollywood
California 91602-2499

WORLD EVENTS, INC.

1413 Lake Ridge Lane
Atlanta, Georgia 30338
770-454-8821 FX 770-454-0296
worldevents@mindspring.com

August 1, 2003

Dear Ron,

With the passing of Bob Hope last Sunday, I know many of us are reflecting on what an incredible life he led and how many of us have been so touched by him. I know that you have wonderful memories with your personal encounters with him. Thank you for sharing those stories with me.

I also wanted to take a moment and thank you again, Ron, for the incredible opportunity that you gave me when you invited me to sing at the reception for Mr. Hope at the Fox Theatre in 1986. After spending years in and out of Vietnam, you knew how much it meant to me that this evening was being dedicated to Vietnam Veterans and that I was able to be a part of it. I have to admit, I was very nervous and fearful that I would forget the words when he unexpectedly jumped up on stage and had me sing to him. I prayed that I wouldn't forget the words of his signature song as he kept smiling and asking me if I was one of the Goldiggers that traveled with his tour. He kept making me laugh. He was so full of energy and warmth for the crowd that gathered to meet him including the Governor. His performance that evening in the theatre, to a packed house, was just the best. The audience was loving him as much as he was loving them.

It's ironic that only two weeks ago, I was invited to do a video interview for the Veteran's History Project which is archiving first hand wartime stories of veterans and civilians for the Library of Congress. One of the questions was, "Why did you want to do USO Shows"? I told them that Bob Hope was my inspiration. When I was growing up in North Hollywood, I watched Mr. Hope's annual Christmas USO Shows on TV year after year and dreamed of going on a tour someday. Then I read his book, " I Owe Russia $1,200" and that made me want to go and perform overseas even more. Finally after 2 years of doing local USO Shows in California, I traveled on my first overseas USO Tour to the Far East and a second to Alaska. I experienced first hand why Mr. Hope loved performing for these great service people away from home especially at Christmas time. I dreamed of seeing his show and I finally did on Christmas day 1968 in DaNang along with 10,000 GI's. I had been in country for 14 months and had just had major emergency surgery and I knew what it felt like to be in that audience and have a touch of home come to us. It was a great show, too. I kept watching the audience and how he made them laugh and how much they loved him. Then, in 1969 after I returned to L.A, I met him at the check in counter at the airport. I was escorting Gypsy Rose Lee to the airport for her last USO Tour to Vietnam. I was working in the Hollywood USO Overseas Office at the time. I had my friend take Gypsy to the gate while I checked in her luggage and at the counter I found myself standing next to Mr. Hope. He was so gracious and I had the opportunity to tell him how much I enjoyed seeing his show in DaNang. I also realized that he was in first class and Gypsy was in coach, as the USO was always on a tight budget. This was a commercial flight to Hawaii where she was to pick up her MAC flight to Vietnam. I asked him if there were any empty seats in first class would he please invite her up to sit with him and he said he would. I later heard that he did and I was so glad. I liked her a lot and I knew she was ill and this would be her last trip. I'm sure it meant a lot to her.

VIETNAM SPECIAL FLIGHT, INC.

Page 2

The USO shows were a beginning for me as an entertainer, Ron, that led to also being a flight attendant and flying troops to Vietnam for 2 years and then returning to Vietnam for 14 months to entertain again. I'm grateful that I had the opportunity to share my stories with the Veterans History Project and with the TV Show M*A*S*H. As you already know, the opening double episode for the tenth season of M*A*S*H was based on my stories and was a tribute to USO entertainers. It was a way for me to say thank you to the wonderful people involved in those stories and to honor other entertainers that did this work, too.

So, Ron, I thank you so much, for giving me such a wonderful memory of singing to the man who inspired me to spread my wings and go for my dream to entertain the troops during Vietnam. He inspired me and many others simply by example by what he did for so many. He lived his passion to live life to the fullest and to give laughter and entertain. He will be so missed but never forgotten.

Take care and I hope to see you soon,

Forever Grateful,

Marina

Marina Alden Bryant, CMP
President
World Events, Inc.

Chapter 7

Vice President Dick Cheney

NEWT Gingrich of Georgia was elected to the House of Representatives in the 1970s, the Speaker of the Georgia House had a visceral dislike of Congressman Gingrich and proceeded to gerrymander him out of his district. Newt looked around for a conservative district and found it in Cobb County, where I lived. U.S. Senator Mack Mattingly called and asked me if I would assist Newt in his new district, and I agreed.

Dick Cheney came to Marietta and gave a speech on behalf of Newt's efforts, I was there and was very impressed by Mr. Cheney's speech. He hit all the right buttons for me and shortly after I sent him a letter and encouraged him to run for higher office which he eventually did.

He was a staff member in the Nixon Administration, Chief of Staff for President Ford, elected to Congress from Wyoming and became Secretary of Defense under President Bush (41). During the early years of the Georgia Vietnam Veterans Leadership Program, we worked hard to convince the Atlanta Braves, Hawks and Falcons to let us participate in their events. This was a perfect way to let Vietnam Veterans know of our available services. As a non-profit organization we could deliver events such as the Golden Knights Parachute Team jumping into the stadium and bring celebrities like James Brown to sing the National Anthem at a Braves game.

I made contact with the Secretary of Defense and invited him to throw out the first pitch at a July 4th Atlanta Braves game, which we dedicated to the Veterans of the first Gulf War. It was an afternoon game, the Braves called and asked if he could come in early and have lunch with the Executives of the Braves and some of the business leaders of Atlanta.'

Secretary Cheney agreed and the luncheon was scheduled at noon in the Atlanta Stadium Private Club. I was also told that Ted Turner was planning to attend. At the time Ted was married to Jane Fonda, which set off alarm bells for me. I was sure the media would be invited and I could just see the morning papers with pictures of Secretary of Defense Cheney, Ted and Jane.

No one from Cheney's office mentioned it, but I knew I had to make sure they were not photographed together. I worked it out with the Braves in a confidential manner. Ted and Jane did in fact attend the luncheon, after wards our party left and went to a private box directly behind home plate.

Just prior to the start of the game, it started raining extremely hard, the game had to be called off; however we did manage to get on the field briefly and Secretary Cheney was able to throw out the first pitch.

I met him on a couple of occasions later when he was Vice President with President Bush (43). I managed to get his personal fax number at his office and we corresponded many times. I had been asked by several friends to intercede with the Vice President on behalf of the two Border Agents, Ramos and Compean who were in a Federal prison for shooting an illegal immigrant who was smuggling drugs across the Mexican border. President Bush did commute their sentences, we had hoped for a pardon, but at least they were released from prison.

The media, as usual made it their life's mission to destroy Vice President Cheney during his eight years as Vice President. History will also make the decision that he was a strong advocate of protecting us against other terrorist attacks on our homeland. He knew that he would become the proverbial punching bag for the Administration, it did not faze him. He simply paid them no attention. He did his job as he saw it and will be remembered as a steady hand during difficult times.

FAX:

12-2-8

VICE PRESIDENT AND MRS CHENEY:

HERE'S WISHING YOU AND YOURS A BLESSED AND HAPPY
CHRISTMAS SEASON. THANKS FOR STAYING THE COURSE
AND KEEPING US SAFE ON OUR SOIL FOR THE PAST 8
YEARS.
WE ASK YOU AGAIN TO ASSIST US IN CONVINCING
PRESIDENT BUSH TO PARDON THE TWO BORDER GUARDS,
RAMOS AND COMPEAN. THEY REMAIN IN SOLITARY
CONFINEMENT AND IF NOT PARDONED WILL REMAIN THERE
AS LONG AS THEY ARE IN PRISON BECAUSE OF THEIR LAW
ENFORCEMENT BACKGROUND. THEY HAVE PAID THEIR
DUES AND A PARDON IS VERY MUCH NEEDED FOR THEM AND
THEIR FAMILIES.
GOD SPEED:

RON MILLER-HOST OF JULY 4TH, ATLANTA BRAVES GAME,
WHILE YOU WERE SEC DEF.

THE VICE PRESIDENT
WASHINGTON

February 15, 2008

Dear Ron:

I enjoyed reading your recollections of past campaigns and thank
you for your kind words of support. I will pass along your
recommendation for Presidential pardons to President Bush for his
consideration.

Lynne and I send our warm regards.

Sincerely,

Dick Cheney

Mr. Ron Miller
3500 Bolt Boulevard
Jonesboro, Arkansas 72401-8029

Chapter 8

General William C. Westmoreland

ENERAL Westmoreland was born in Spartanburg, South Carolina. He attended The Citadel for a year before transferring to West Point. He held the highest command position in the cadet corps. It was standard policy to allow the Corps to pick their Commencement Speaker. General Westmoreland led the efforts to invite the famous General "Blackjack" Pershing to be their speaker. As the top cadet, General Westmoreland was presented a sword by the General, he still has the sword.

General Westmoreland commanded U.S. Forces during the Vietnam War from 1964 to 1968. I never had the opportunity to meet or see the General during my three tours as a helicopter pilot, but it was obvious that the men and women who served there had a lot of respect for him. Unfortunately the Vietnam War was the first war that was basically run by the politicians in Washington, D.C. This was especially true with President Johnson who had a model of Khe Sanh built and placed in the war room of the White House.

General Westmoreland understood that we would never defeat the enemy in the South as long as we gave them sanctuary in Cambodia, Laos and North Vietnam. He asked repeatedly to attack the enemy in their base camps in those areas and approval never came.

Then came my opportunity to meet him while he was still on active duty. I was the Operations Officer at Gray Army Airfield at Fort Lewis, Washington. We received notice he would fly into our airfield, then fly by Huey to the Boeing Plant in Seattle. General Westmoreland had gone to the Command Flight School to learn how to fly helicopters. An instructor pilot was always required to be the Aircraft Commander on all flights by General Officers. A Chief Warrant Officer and I were selected as the crew.

General Westmoreland arrived, boarded the helicopter and flew it to Seattle and back, he was a very good pilot. I had a great picture taken with him and when he came to Atlanta, I showed him the picture. He remembered the flight and signed it for me.

He retired as Chief of Staff of the Army in 1972 and made his life work traveling in all 50 states to lecture and participate in Veterans' activities. That is how I became involved with him, a relationship that lasted for over 20 years. He came to Atlanta to speak to a Veteran group, I introduced myself as the Executive Director, Ga. Vietnam Veterans Leadership Program. He looked at my card and said, "This is a great nationwide effort that has done more for Vietnam Veterans than all the rest put together." He said he would be available to assist us, just give him a call.

We took him up on his offer and brought him to Georgia many times to assist us in our work. He was the Grand Marshal of our Veterans Day Parade and speaker at our evening banquet. He participated in numerous events honoring Veterans. He dedicated Memorials in several locations in Georgia, and I had the great honor of being his Aide-de-Camp during his trips.

I invited General Westmoreland and his wife, Kitsey, to the Bob Hope special, he accepted, and we sent him airline tickets. Unfortunately, he had to cancel. He sent Mr. Hope a note expressing regret that he could not attend. Mr. Hope sent me another personal letter saying he had hoped his good friend, Westy, could make it but understood.

In 1982, General Westmoreland filed a $120 million law suit against CBS over a documentary, "A Vietnam Deception," which implied he had deceived President Johnson and the public about enemy troop strength in Vietnam. After an 18 week trial in New York, the case was settled shortly before it was to go to trial. Westy felt vindicated. Our old friends at CBS was up to their old tricks, remember the dust-up with CBS and President Bush, that resulted in the firing of Dan Rather .

General Westmoreland died at the age of 91 and was buried at the West Point Cemetery. In 2007, I was invited by my good friend, Dallas Wood, a retired LTC that was a classmate at Arkansas State University. He was a trustee at ASU and invited me to join him on a trip to West Point for a football game. We lost but won against them when they came to Arkansas to play us. West Point treated us as VIP's, we attended a reception, luncheon, briefing and tour of the incredible grounds at The Point.

I had the opportunity to break away, our host drove me to the Cemetery. I asked the Director if I could visit the grave of General Westmoreland and he personally escorted me to the site. The former Superintendents of West Point are buried in one area and their markers are in a circle facing inwards. I took several pictures, the Director said, "You may wonder why we have them in a circle facing each other.' I replied, "Yes!" He replied, "They are auguring over who was the best Superintendent"'

As I mentioned in the Chapters about Perfume River and the POW documentary, we came up with a very good idea. We had made excellent contacts in Vietnam and filmed Senior General Giap, the Defense Minister who spoke highly of General Westmoreland and his conduct of the war. We met with General Westmoreland in SC and proposed to him the idea of bringing General Giap to the US for the purpose of doing a Documentary. He agreed and we sent a letter to our contacts in Vietnam. Much to our surprise, General Giap agreed, we were ecstatic and started the ball rolling. We contacted a very reputable Production Company in Atlanta and they agreed to do the documentary at their expense and would recoup monies at the sale of the documentary.

Sometime later, we received word that General Giap would not be able to make the trip because of his health, much later we found out that the Politburo had decided not to approve the trip. Of course we were disappointed, but came up with a fall back plan. We had the film with General Giap that we had made during the POW trip to Hanoi. We then asked General Westmoreland if we could film his portion in Charleston, he readily agree and we spent a few days there with him

We interviewed him at a Hotel, the Citadel, a Vietnamese fire base at Patriots Point and the Medal of Honor museum on the carrier Yorktown. I did the interview with the General and toward the end I asked him a question, "If you could change one thing about Vietnam, what would it be"? He thought for awhile and said, " I would not have used body count as a measure of success." It surprised me and later when we thought about it, it made sense. When you fight a guerilla war, you do not have front lines? You do not capture and hold territory, so how do you measure success? I guess that is why they came up with the "body count" method. We are still trying to find a Production Company that will take both interviews and make it into a great documentary. We will never give up, someday it will happen.

In his autobiography, "A Soldier Reports," Westy wrote that in Vietnam, while he tried to avoid any vendetta against the press, he sometimes resented the time he had to spend correcting "errors, misinterpretations, judgments and falsehoods" contained in news reports. But he wrote that the press is "...such a bulwark of the American system, that it is well to allow some mistakes and derelictions to make every effort to assure that total freedom and independence continue to exist."

Sadly to say, if he were alive today, he may not be so generous. The media does not report the news today, they make it with their lock-step support for liberal causes, which in my humble opinion is why they are going broke.

General Westmoreland was cut from old cloth, he was an extremely honest, courteous and patriotic individual who loved his wife, his country and his family. He was an Eagle Scout, a fact that he was very proud of. He was a great leader, a tremendous supporter of the Military and Veterans. I am very proud and humbled to call him my friend.

To Ron,
with all regards and
best wishes,

Nov. '85

VIETNAM SPECIAL FLIGHT, INC.

Vì hòa bình
vì hữu nghị

giữa
nhân dân Mỹ và
Việt nam

26/3/93

March 26, 1993
Ron Miller meets with Senior
General Vo Nguyen Giap (North
Vietnam Defence Minister) The
Opera House, Hanoi, Vietnam
Translation of above inscription
"Peace and Reconciliation for
all American and Vietnamese
Veterans and their Countries"
(NEXT TO MILLER -- MARY "T" + ALEX
WELLS)

General VO NGUYEN GIAP
30 Hoang Dieu Street
Ha Noi – Vietnam

September 26, 1993

Mr. RON MILLER
Executive Director
Georgia Veterans Leadership Program, Inc.
825 Fairfield Drive
Marietta, Georgia 30068
(404) 565 - 8444

Dear Mr. Ron Miller,

I have received your letter of August 14, 1993.

Reading your letter, I learn that General William C. Westmoreland, the United States Congressional Medal of Honor Society and the TET Vietnam Reconciliation Project wish to invite me and my wife to meet with General William C. Westmoreland and the U.S Congressional Medal and Honor Society, during the period of the 22-28 October 1993 in Charleston, South Carolina.

First of all, I welcome the above mentioned initiative by the U.S Congressional Medal of Honor Society, the TET Vietnam Reconciliation Project and yourself.

I really appreciate if you could convey my thanks to General William C. Westmoreland for his invitation and goodwill. I also want to ask you to convey my thanks to Senator Sam Nunn.

However, it is regrettable to let you know that I could not go to South Carolina for such a meeting due to my previous engagements which could not be changed.

In my interview in Ha Noi last March for the first part titled "Vietnam POW's : The Final Healing" of your TET reconciliation documentary, I said it was time for the Vietnamese and American people to look forward and build good relationship.

I believe that the TET reconciliation documentary will contribute to further mutual understanding between the two peoples—and accelerate the normalization process of relations between our two countries.

Once again, thank you all for your gracious invitation. Please accept my wife's and my best wishes.

May friendly relations and cooperation for the sake of our two peoples interest be forthcoming.

Sincerely,

General VO NGUYEN GIAP (signed)

Chapter 9

Governor Mike Huckabee

MY first contact with Governor Huckabee occurred at Senator Bob Dole's National Campaign Headquarters in Washington, D.C., in 1995. I was sitting in my office, when someone stuck his head in and informed me that the Lt. Governor of Arkansas, Mike Huckabee, was visiting the Headquarters. I made my way to the main office and introduced myself. I told him that my brother, Owen Miller, was a State Representative and he told me that he knew him well. We made some small talk for a few minutes, it was approaching lunch time, I asked him if he had any plans for lunch, he replied no and I invited him to join me at Union Station which was located a couple blocks from the office.

We had a very good visit, we talked about politics in Arkansas for some time and the conversation finally came around to his political career. He told me about the special election for Lt. Governor which he won. The Democrats were very unhappy that he won and literally nailed the door to the office closed; so he could not report to work.

The Governor is one of the most astute politicians that I have ever met, instead of making a big fuss about his treatment, he found a very small table, a metal chair and placed it at the front door. He made a hand lettered sign that read, Lt. Governor Mike Huckabee and sat in the chair. There was no way the media could ignore this, they covered the event and the Democrats had egg all over their face. They relented, opened the door and let the Lt. Gov. in to conduct his business.

In July 1996 he became Governor when his predecessor resigned. He was one of the youngest Governors in the Country at the time. He then was elected to a full-four year term as Governor in 1998, then re-elected to another full term in 2002. He served as our Governor for ten and a half years and when he left office our State had a billion dollar surplus. When this book is published, it will probably be zero..

I was visiting a good friend in Atlanta in the later part of 2006, Norm Cates is the owner and publisher of the national newspaper, The Club Insider, which is directed to the Health and Fitness Industry. Norm was very impressed with Governor Huckabee, both he and the Governor had lost 110 pounds. Norm said he would love to interview

Governor Huckabee for his newspaper. I told him I would make contact with the Governor and see if I could set it up. He agreed and we planned to interview him at the Governor's mansion.

Norm and I stayed at the Little Rock Peabody Hotel the night before the interview, and Norm worked on questions for the Governor, and he came up with a dozen questions about health and fitness.

We arrived at the Mansion and were escorted into a room in the private living area. The Governor walked in, and an hour later, we completed the session and walked outside to depart for the hotel. Norm remarked, "I am very surprised at his knowledge of the issues, it was the best interview that I have conducted." The Governor did not refer to any notes during the interview.

Governor Huckabee completed four years college in two and a half years. He is one of the most educated and astute politician that I have ever met.

He came in second to Senator McCain for the Republican nomination for President in 2008, with a fraction of the funds available.

He has written six books, the last is titled, "Do The Right Thing" which spent its first weeks of release in the top 10 of the New York Times bestseller list.

I was honored that Governor Huckabee asked me to join with him during his run for the presidency as his Veterans Adviser. He is a very strong supporter of our Military and Veterans, and you can see his Veterans Bill of Rights in his new book.

I have met his great family, they are indeed an All-American family and it is my hope the Governor elects to run for President again in 2011 This great Country needs his wisdom, especially at this time in our history.

GOVERNOR MIKE HUCKABEE'S VETERANS BILL OF RIGHTS

We owe the men and women who have stepped forward in defense of our nation our eternal gratitude for their service. They have earned our respect and appreciation and deserve our support after they leave the services. The following Bill of Rights will assist them as they leave the Armed Forces and integrate back into civilian life.

1. Veterans Administration Health Care Funding should be mandatory

2. A comprehensive GI Bill that provides full tuition, books, fees and living expenses at any institution to which the veteran is accepted

3. Allocate the necessary funds to determine a veterans disability claim to less than 6 months.

4. All disabled military retirees should receive both their military retirement and VA Compensation

5. Veterans Administration should be able to collect and retain Medicare dollars for treatment of Non-Service Connected Medicare eligible veterans

6. Veterans should be provided employment and training opportunities at the Federal, State and Local level.

7. National Guard and Reserve personnel mobilized for service should be given the same services as the Active Armed Forces.

8. The fullest possible accounting of the fate of America's POW/MIAs

9. Make sure all veterans are aware of the benefits and services due them.

10. Employment, training and veterans preference in hiring should be available at the Federal, State and Local level.

11. Three Percent contracts and subcontracts with Federal Agencies for disabled veteran-owned businesses should be required by all Federal Agencies.

12. All homeless veterans should have access to suitable housing and subsistence.

13. Funds should be made available to the U.S. Small Business Administration for Direct SBA Loans to veterans.

14. Adequate funds should be made available for state of the art Mental Health Treatment for veterans.

Mike Huckabee

Dear Ron—

Thanks for the ride and the lunch — it was great visiting with you, and I'll call Owen soon.

I look forward to working with you to elect "President Dole."[4]

Best wishes, Mike Huckabee

Chapter 10

Winthrop Paul Rockefeller

WHEN I returned to my home-state of Arkansas in 2004, I immediately got involved in local and state politics. I agreed to work as the Regional Chairman, Veterans for Bush/Cheney and was invited to the Veterans for Bush kickoff announcement in Little Rock. The announced speakers were Lt. Governor Rockefeller and a Retired Army General Officer.

During my first tour as a Helicopter Pilot in Vietnam, I had been awarded the first of the two Distinguished Flying Crosses during 1966. The story had appeared in the local newspapers where I lived in Arkansas. Sometime later, my mother received a letter from Governor Winthrop Rockefeller, a World War II Veteran congratulating me on the award. I shared that story with Lt. Governor Rockefeller and he asked me if I would send him a copy of the letter. He mentioned that he collected letters written by his dad for his family's archives. I immediately sent him the letter.

In 2005, Lt. Gov. Rockefeller announced that he would run for Governor and I immediately sign on for the campaign. We were all very excited about his prospects and the campaign was under way.

I attended a fundraiser in Jonesboro for Rockefeller, I wore my miniature Master Army Aviator wings in the lapel of my sports coat, Rockefeller noticed them and asked me what aircraft I flew. I told him helicopters and Beechcraft multi-engine airplanes. He asked me which Beechcraft I liked the most. I responded, "The Baron! It's the sports car of the Beechcraft." He told me that he owned a Baron and enjoyed flying it very much. A standard question one pilot asked another in a situation like this is, "How many hours do you have?" He responded, that he did not know, he did not keep a log. Later I realized that a Billionaire does not have to keep a log. Why should they? He asked me what I did and I responded that I was on the National Advisory Committee, Veterans Business Affairs, U.S. Small Business Administration.

He said he had received a letter from a plane manufacture near where I lived, the individual was seeking assistance in expanding his business and asked for Rockefeller's help. He asked me if I would visit with him, look at his business and report back to him. I did, the businessman had an excellent business plan to expand and the demand seemed to be there for the product. I reported back to Rockefeller my findings.

Shortly after that, Rockefeller became ill with a blood disorder, which if left untreated could develop into leukemia. He underwent two bone marrow transplants at a Seattle Hospital and died in July 2006. Asa Hutchinson, a former U.S. Attorney and U.S. Congressman, was the primary winner and was defeated by Governor Mike Beebe.

Governor Beebe is on record as saying, "If Rockefeller had lived, he would probably would have been elected Governor!" We all agreed. Rockefeller would have made a superb Governor!

On October 9, 2010 the Craighead County Republican Committee in Jonesboro, Arkansas, held their 2nd Annual Reagan Day Round-Up, an event that raises money to assist our Local, State and Congressional Candidates in the final push of the 2010 campaign. Our candidate for the U.S. Senate, Congressman John Boozman, R-AR, could not attend, and he sent Will Rockefeller to speak on his behalf.

Will is the son of the former Lt.Gov. of Arkansas, Win Rockefeller. His Grandfather was Governor Winthrop Rockefeller who was Governor of Arkansas in the 1960's. Governor Rockefeller served in combat in the U.S. Army during World War II and was awarded the Purple Heart, Bronze Star and other awards for his service. He was an outstanding Governor of our State.

I heard Will Rockefeller speak once before at a large gathering at the WinRock Farms on top of Petit Jean Mountain near Little Rock. He is a very effective speaker and has a bright future in Arkansas Politics.

I decided to present him with the letter that Governor Rockefeller sent to my Mother in 1967, congratulating me on the award of the Distinguished Flying Cross and thanking me and my family for our service during the Vietnam War. He looked at it, then told me that he could not accept it because it obviously meant a great deal to me. I assured him it was a copy, and he then accepted it with his appreciation. There is no doubt that Will Rockefeller's name will be known in a few years to many people, he is an exceptional young man who will do great things.

WINTHROP ROCKEFELLER
GOVERNOR

October 31, 1967

Maj. Ronald Miller
c/o Mr. and Mrs. A. M. Miller
Payneway Community
Trumann, Arkansas 72472

Dear Major Miller:

I know my fellow Arkansans share with me
a deep feeling of pride in the recognition of
your bravery in Vietnam by your being awarded
the Distinguished Flying Cross.

It is my hope that the sacrifices made
by you and other American servicemen will
inspire all of us to work harder toward that
time when we will all live at peace with our
fellowmen.

With all good wishes,

Sincerely,

Winthrop Rockefeller
Governor

Chapter 11

Senator John McCain

I have had the opportunity to work with Senator McCain on several campaigns and other events. In the early 80's, when he was still a Congressman, I invited him to Atlanta to be our Grand Marshal for the huge Veterans Day Parade and Luncheon on Veterans Day. He agreed and was very well received by the Veterans and citizens in Georgia.

After the Parade, he was our keynote speaker for the Veterans Day luncheon at a major hotel in downtown Atlanta, he made a very good speech and opened up the floor for questions afterward. One Vietnam Veteran, who was concerned about some of the Congressman's stand on the POW/MIA issue, asked him a question that seemed to question his total support for the issue and the possibility that we might have left some Prisoners behind. We saw a flash of anger in Congressman McCain that we had not expected or witnessed before.

Afterwards when we were alone, he apologized to me for his response, I told him, he had nothing to apologize for, he did a great job and we appreciated him for his service and especially taking the time to be with us in Atlanta.

Not too long after that, we invited Senator Goldwater R-AZ to come to Georgia and assist in the campaign to re-elect Senator Mack Mattingly to the U.S. Senate. I had taken a leave of absence from the GVVLP to work on his campaign. I had the great satisfaction of spending some quality time with Senator Goldwater, who was a major leader of the Conservative wing of the Republican Party. Senator Goldwater had announcement his retirement from politics and Congressman McCain was running for his seat. I asked Senator Goldwater if he thought McCain would win the seat, Goldwater replied, "The race is his to lose!" Senator McCain did indeed win the Senate seat and holds it today. Just so happened, a photographer snapped a photo of me asking Goldwater the question, I sent it to him, he autographed it, it now occupies a place of honor in my office .

Later, I was the Coalition Director for the re-election of Senator Paul Coverdell R-GA. The campaign had invited Senator McCain to visit the state and campaign for Senator Coverdell. We planned a fly-around of the state primarily to participate in news conferences, meet with editors of the local newspapers and some Veteran events.

Our mode of travel was a private six-passenger Beechcraft King-Air, a very nice airplane which I was qualified to fly. When we boarded the airplane, Marine General Ray Davis was seated in the rear seat, across the aisle from Senator McCain. We took off and General Davis turned to the Senator and told him that he Commanded the 3d Marine Division in Vietnam and had invited McCain's dad, Admiral John McCain, the Commander of Naval Operations, Pacific to have lunch with him on a mountain top in General Davis's area. Admiral McCain accepted, they had lunch and General Davis told McCain that the last time he saw him, he was saluting his departure from the mountain top.

I watched McCain throughout the conversation, he became a little emotional and remarked, "I think of him everyday" It was a remarkable moment.

The day's activities went very well, Senator Coverdell was elected to the Senate, the first Republican to be re-elected to the US Senate from Georgia since reconstruction.

Senator McCain was a strong supporter of Senator Dole, he traveled with him some and spoke to Veteran groups on Dole's behalf. I had the pleasure of working with Senator McCain from time to time during 1995 and 1996.

Senator McCain had always planned to run for the Presidency, he ran in 2000 against President Bush (41). When the polls indicated he did not have a chance, he dropped out and supported President Bush.

He threw his hat in the ring again for the 2008 race, won the primary and lost to Senator Obama. I knew a couple of the Veteran leaders in Senator McCain's headquarters. They asked me to get involved in the primary, but I had to decline because I had agreed to work for Governor Huckabee. After the Senator won the Primary, I became the State Chairman, Veterans for McCain/Palin in Arkansas. Although we carried Arkansas by a 60-40 margin for Senator McCain, we lost the big one.

As of the writing of this book, it appears that the American people made a huge mistake, only time will tell.

On March 28, 2009 this editorial appeared in *The Jonesboro Sun*, our local newspaper. It was titled "Slighting Veterans." It did not take long for President Obama and his Administration to show their true colors with regard to the men and women who have stepped forward in defense of our great Country. Take a seat, folks, you may not believe what the President is planning for those Veterans who were wounded during their service. Mind you, these courageous servicemen and women are volunteers, some of the best and brightest among us.

The Commander-In-Chief called the Commanders of The American Legion, Veterans of Foreign Wars, the Disabled American Veterans and others to the White House and dropped a bomb in their laps. The Administration is planning on requiring our service-connected disabled veterans to use their private medical insurance policies to pay the Veterans Administration for their treatment. This is simply unconscionable. Private insurance companies did not send our men and women into harm's way, the government did, and it is responsible for caring for those who have been wounded, period.

If our disabled veterans are required to use their family insurance plan, it would surely raise their premiums beyond affordable rates. The veteran would max out his policy quickly, and the rest of the family would not have any health insurance.

The new Secretary of the Veterans Administration was asked about is, and he confirmed that the plan was to be considered.

This is an outrage, this from an Administration who is giving away trillions of dollars to the greedy and giving the shaft to our injured troops. All Americans should get involved quickly. Call the White House! Call your elected officials! Tell them to stop this madness now!

JOHN McCAIN
CHAIRMAN

RONALD REAGAN
FOUNDER

Chapter 12

Movie: Perfume River

WHEN I started the Georgia Vietnam Veterans Leadership Program, Inc., Mike Mantegna, a lawyer and member of our Board of Directors offered me free office space in his Law Office. Not only did I have a nice office, but had access to his very proficient Secretary. After a couple years, I decided to move my office into my home, the employment office operated by Tony Hamilton was located at the Atlanta Vet Center and the Small Business Program was run by Andy Farris out of his home office.

My office was located in the front part of my home. From my desk, I could see the driveway and street. Easy to get to work, just walk down the hall and turn right. Not only that, I had immediate access to the swimming pool and hot tub, which I used quite frequently. Traffic in Atlanta became a nightmare and its much worse now; so my life was much less stressful, I hate traffic, lost time, lost money and terrible drivers.

I was sitting at my desk when a car pulled into my driveway, one that I did not recognize. A couple walked to my front door, I thought, jeez, I hope they are not selling anything. Had I not been visible to them, I probably would not have answered the door bell. Mary Thibaudeau and Alex Wells Jr., husband and wife introduced themselves and said, "Someone told us that if you wanted to know anything about Vietnam Veterans in the Atlanta area, contact Ron Miller."

They proceeded to tell me about a screenplay they had written with the title of "Perfume River," a large river that begins in China and runs west to east across Vietnam and empties into the South China Sea. The river cuts through the ancient city of Hue, Vietnam which was their Imperial Capital for centuries. The screenplay is based on a true story about Alex and his experiences in Vietnam during the TET 1968 battle, which was a battle that changed the Vietnam War and the American people's attitude toward it. It was the beginning of the end of the War.

Alex's Mom had paid for a one month visit to New York City, where they teamed up with a script doctor to put the finishing touches to the screenplay. They gave me a verbal synopsis of the script, asked me to read it and give them my thoughts and reaction.

I thought, here we go again, several people over the years had given me songs, articles and a couple screenplays to read, they were all bad. I started reading this one and did not put it down until I finished it.

While the central theme is about Vietnam, it's much more than a war movie; it has intrigue, mystery, action, betrayal, reconciliation and friendship. To be honest, it left me in tears. I contacted Alex and Mary and told them that I was very impressed with the story and would help them anyway I can. The date was August 1988.

It is now 2009 and we are still out there fighting to get this story told. Our continuing saga reminds me of a Carl Sandburg quote, "Nothing happens ... but first a dream." Well we have our dream and we will not give up.

Alex joined the Marine Corps and was in Officer Training at Quantico, Virginia. The South Vietnamese military sent two Vietnamese captains to go through the training course. They assigned both to Alex; it was called the "buddy system." It was Alex's responsibility to assist them in their training, studying and social activities. One of the officers was from a Mandarin family, a very successful Vietnamese family with wealth; the other was from a peasant family. His father had fought against the French.

Another member of this training unit was named Fred Smith, who became the Founder, Chairman and Chief Executive Office of Federal Express, he had graduated from Yale and joined the Marine Corps to become an officer like Alex. Alex was a jock. He was the runner up to the National Wrestling Champion in his weight class at the University of Virginia. The other members of the unit called Alex, the jock and Fred, Yalie.

We started working the script in earnest, we found out that Mr. Smith owned the production company, ALCON in Hollywood, their first film *My Dog Skip* was a huge success, other films included *Racing Stripes, Sisterhood of the Traveling Pants, Insomnia* and others.

Fred Smith served two tours in Vietnam. He was a Marine grunt his first tour and was an FO his second year. He left the Corps and the rest is history. One interesting point, he knew his concept of FedEx would work, he traveled to Little Rock, AR, and presented it to the business leaders there and asked for assistance in forming the Company, they declined, he went to Memphis and they agreed to partner with him, FedEx is now the largest cargo delivery system in the

World. Mr. Smith wrote his thesis at Yale on the concept of his company, the pin head Professor gave him a C- and said it would never work. I gave General Ray Davis our script to read, told him about Mr. Smith's ownership of ALCON and asked him if he would send a letter and introduce us and Perfume River. He responded, as he always did when I asked him for assistance, he said, "by all means."

I wrote the letter, General Davis signed it and we sent it to Mr. Smith, a few days later we received a letter from Mr. Smith, he had just reviewed a book about the famous Marine General, Chesty Puller, there was a chapter about General Davis included. Mr. Smith told us to send the script to him and his Production Company in LA.

They liked the script, told us it was too long and to reduce it considerably, which we did. Next ALCON invited Mary T., Alex and myself to come to LA for a meeting with them and several of the talent agencies to gage their response to the script. They paid all expenses, we met and briefed the agencies and left with a good feeling.

As I mentioned early in the book, when Bob Hope passed away, I was invited to the funeral services and was encouraged to attend an "important" meeting about the script, a major mistake on my part and one I regret to this day.

A couple years earlier, I sent Mr. Hope a copy of the script, we also told him that we wanted to include a USO show in the movie and asked him if he would consider working with us. I received a prompt reply from Mr. Hope. He told me that he would give the script to a couple of readers and that he would consider working with us. What a prince of a man.

We were told early on that the chance of getting a movie made in Hollywood was almost impossible, and we were beginning to believe them. We would receive encouragement from time to time and we kept plugging along.

We met Shelby Gregory an actor in Hollywood who would put us in contact with Attorney Jack Merrick a former Producer who left the movie world and now owns a company in the medical field. He became our agent and has worked tirelessly on the project, like us, he thinks it will be an outstanding movie.

Apparently ALCON did not think the script would be a viable product in its current form or it would have been made by now.

Mr. Merrick told us his brother-in-law, Steve Peters, who is a top screenwriter, he wrote "Wild Things," staring Kevin Bacon and has a very good reputation in the business. Mr. Merrick sent him the script, he really liked the story and agreed to re-write the script from page one to make it more attractive to the Hollywood suits. He did and it is a much better script, the main story is there, but it reads much better.

The script was sent back to ALCON, they are now considering asking Mr. Peters to improve Alex's part in order to attract a top Hollywood star.

ALCON's latest movie was "Blindside," which was a blockbuster and at last count had grossed over $300 million dollars. On July 23rd, Alex, Mary T. and I signed an option with ALCON to make "Perfume River."

Stay tuned folks, watch for, "Perfume River," at a theater near you in the future. It will be one helluva a movie.

Chapter 13

POW Documentary

Beyond Courage:
Surviving Vietnam As A POW

IN 1992 the three of us, Mary T., Alex and I discussed the possibilities of making a documentary with some of the returned Vietnam POWs. I had met a few of the POWs including Senator John McCain, Orson Swindle, Ben Purcell and others. We put together an excellent group, raised the necessary funds and got approval from Vietnam. Dr. Tran K. Van, a former housing Minister in South Vietnam under President Thieu, who managed to escape when the North captured Saigon agreed to be our liaison with the Vietnamese Government. Since 1975 Dr. Van has returned to Vietnam more than 40 times and was well connected with the Hanoi government and uniquely qualified to assist in the documentary.

Now we turned our efforts on raising the necessary funds to pay the expenses for the trip. Again we were lucky to find a Production Company in Los Angeles who was willing to film the documentary at no charge up front, they would be paid after the Documentary was sold. We ended up with 14 individuals on the trip, the three of us, three Production staff, six POWs, wife of one and daughter of another.

Again, we were lucky in finding an individual in New York City that would fund the trip, if any money was made, we would repay the loan. The benefactor told us he was not concerned about getting his money back, he just wanted to be a part of the effort.

We selected six POWs, Commander Everett Alvarez Jr. USN, Ret., Colonel Leo Thorsness, USAF, Ret., Colonel Fred Cherry, USAF Ret., Colonel Ben Purcell, USA, Ret., Dat Nguyen, a South Vietnamese Pilot and Bernhardt Diehl, a German Medical Aid Worker. Leo's wife Gaylee and Ben's daughter Joy made the trip, we wanted to get their story of coping with their loved one being held as a POW for a long period of time.

Hundreds of American planes were shot down during the Vietnam War in the 1960s. Those Aviators were taken prisoner in North Vietnam and were faced with the most intense, sustained battle of the war. They lived in a world of agony closed to public scrutiny. Brutalized, kept in the dark and isolated from each other, these heroic men were tested to their very core. Yet, somehow they survived the torture.

For the first time, cameras were allowed to go inside the infamous Hanoi Hilton, a rat infested, run down prison where the prisoners lived. The Hanoi Hilton was scheduled to be torn down shortly after we left and the POWs and family members were allowed to document what happened during the longest wartime captivity in U.S. history.

U.S. Navy pilot Commander Everett Alvarez Jr. was shot down over North Vietnam on the first day of the air war over the north, and held for eight and one half years. Alvarez and his fellow POWS were forced to live in a world of total silence, unable to communicate with each other through the thick walls until one day they discovered an ingenious tap code. The tight community they formed provided the foundation for surviving the constant torture and harsh life.

USAF pilot Colonel Leo Thorsness was a hot-shot U.S. fighter pilot, and received the nation's highest honor for his heroism, the Medal of Honor, for actions before he was shot down. In prison, he was held in a dreaded area of the Hanoi Hilton called 'Heartbreak Hotel', a group of cells that stank of human excess, punctuated with screams of agony. As the war dragged on, Thorsness wondered if he would ever see his home again. To keep hope alive, Thorsness and his cellmates began to 'walk home', ten thousand miles--all inside their tiny cell.

USAF pilot Colonel Fred Cherry was the first African-American pilot shot down, and his captors tortured him mercilessly to make propaganda statements against the United States. But Cherry refused to let his skin color be used as a propaganda weapon, and sustained ninety-three days of continuous torture. He and the other pilots felt that they were all unified as Americans, without color or race--a conviction that helped them withstand the savage treatment. Col. Cherry was awarded the Air Force Cross for his actions in prison, along with thirty-three other medals.

USA Colonel Ben Purcell was captured in South Vietnam and later taken North. He was isolated from the pilots, and spent five years in solitary confinement in a small 6 by 10 foot cell. For three and a half years of those years Purcell did not touch another human being. Strug-

gling to hold on to his sanity, one day he shook the h
known man under his door. That one brief but impo
helped him hang on and keep hope alive. Faith and Go
portant element of every prisoners survival. His steadfast
family and the desire to get home gave him strength to e ....ice.
For each escape, the U.S. Army awarded Col. Purcell a Silver Star and
a Legion of Merit.

Dat Nguyen, a South Vietnamese fighter pilot (A-1E Skyraider)
was shot down over North Vietnam, ironically he was born in North
Vietnam in Hanoi in 1940. He fled to the South with his father at age 3
and fought against his family and friends in the South Vietnamese Air
Force. Dat was the only South Vietnamese pilot to survive captivity in
the North. He had gone to flight school in San Antonio and had a
Texas drivers license and was wearing an Air Force ring. The North
Vietnamese was convinced he was an American and that saved his life.

Bernhard Diehl and four other German humanitarian social workers, two males and three females, were captured by the Viet Cong near
DaNang, South Vietnam in 1967. After a thousand mile hike up the
Ho Chi Minh trail over a three month period he and one other worker
survived and were imprisoned for five years. On the documentary he
stated that he felt victorious over his captors because he survived. "I
don't feel like a hero," he said, "but I do feel like a winner." He is now
a doctor living in Germany.

These men faced their unique nightmare with bravery, determination, ingenuity and integrity. In the camps they tapped strengths they
never dreamed possible-combining faith in God, the love of those back
home and a belief in each other. Their captors never knew it, but in
the darkness and silence, these bold and daring men found a way to
unite, forming a very tight community. The route that took them to
hell and back, they found, was indeed Beyond Courage. In my life
time, I never thought I would be privileged to meet such men, let alone
called them my good friend. My life was enriched beyond belief and I
will   never   forget   my
time spent with these heroes. All have gone on to very productive lives
and have written books about their time spent as a Prisoner-of War:
Chained Eagle by Everett Alvarez Jr., *Love and Duty* by Ben and Anne
Purcell, *Surviving Hell* by Leo Thorsness, *MOH: Two Souls Indivisible*
by Fred Cherry and Porter Halyburton. I strongly recommend you
get these books and read about their extraordinary experiences as a
POW and how they coped and survived.

Our crew was very well received everywhere we went, we were given unprecedented access to all the prison systems, except Son Tay, which is located miles from the capitol, Hanoi. As you may recall, Son Tay was the prison that we attempted a rescue operation with helicopters. When they arrived, it was determined that all the POWs had been moved to other camps.

We had asked for a meeting with Senior General Giap, the Defense Minister of North Vietnam, he was also a prominent member of the Politburo, which ruled their country. We were promised fifteen minutes. When he found out that some of the POWs had their wives and daughters, he gave us an hour and fifteen minutes. Just a few weeks before we arrived he turned down a request by Dan Rathers for an interview.

We were also told that it was the most comprehensive interview that he had given to any American since the end of the war. We specifically asked him about the treatment of our POWs. He told us that the prison camps were not run by the Army, but by a special unit of the Government. We later found out that this was true.

We learned that General Giap's Wife and her Sister had been captured by the French during that war, the Sister was executed and his wife died in prison.

The Producer asked several Vietnamese how they felt about the Americans who they fought against. Some responded, we fought the Chinese for a thousand years, the French a hundred years. We only fought the Americans for ten years, you were short-timers.

We got seventy hours of historical film which included the interview with General Giap, Hanoi Hannah, the Tokyo Rose of Vietnam, and several of the camp commanders and of course detail coverage of the POWs in their respective prisons. Colonel Purcell was never allowed to write or receive letters during the five years that he was a POW. When his daughter, Joy, met General Giap, she asked him why he did not let her father write to his family. General Giap replied that it was his policy to leave those decisions up to the camp commanders.

After we completed the work in Hanoi, all the POWs returned to the United States, except Colonel Ben Purcell and his daughter Joy (Joy was in the TV business in Georgia and she made a great film that has been shown to audiences across Georgia, and she also wrote stories that received wide coverage in newspapers here in the States) and the film crew departed Hanoi for South Vietnam to find the site where Colonel Purcell was shot down.

Our trusted Advisor, Tran Van located the VC Commander for that area and he promised us that he would be able to find the exact location.

We arrived in DaNang, met the guide and started for the location which was near the beach on the South China sea. We parked our vehicles, walked into a village, which reminded me of the ones I saw during my tours in Vietnam. We saw a couple of older gentlemen who were wearing the standard clothing, a large conical hat, made of straw and black pajamas, and looked like VC to *me*.

Our guide told them why we were there, told them about Colonel Purcell and the date he was shot down in the vicinity. These two gentlemen became excited and told us exactly where the helicopter crashed. We walked out of the village toward the beach area and found the site. Col Purcell knew it was the location, because there was a cemetery located nearby. It was quite an emotional trip for Col. Purcell, while there he shared the story of the shoot-down. He and another soldier had been sent to an area to fix some communication equipment, after completed their work they started back to home station, they ran into bad weather and the pilots had to drop down low to keep from flying in the clouds, the local VC opened up on the Huey, hit it several times and it caught on fire. The pilots made an emergency landing, they left the aircraft and set up a defensive position in a large bomb crater. The mechanic, James George, had left his M-16 rifle in the chopper and went back to get it. The aircraft was burning and he was badly burned, but managed to get back to the bomb crater. Eventually, the VC captured all six Americans, the two pilots, two crew chiefs, Colonel Purcell, and the mechanic. After the capture the captors made them take off their boots, used their shoestrings to tie their hands behind their back, and the six men walked all night. When they were allowed to stop to rest the next morning, Ben asked their captors to get help for PFC George. He was told that he was no longer in charge and to move on up the trail with the other 4 men. The captors kept PFC George seated by the trail. As the other 5 men moved on up the trial they heard a gunshot. They were afraid the enemy executed him instead of getting help for him.

As we were leaving DaNang for Saigon for additional filming then back to the United States, Colonel Purcell pulled out his wallet, gave our guide $50, which was a lot of money back then in Vietnam. He asked the VC Commander to try and locate the mechanic's grave site and pass along the information to our POW/MIA recovery teams located in Hanoi.

Toward the end of the war a group of wives and parents formed The National League of Families of American Prisoners and Missing in Southeast Asia for the sole purpose of accounting for those Vietnam Veterans who are still missing in action. As of March 2009, 841 of our fellow Vietnam War Veterans have been recovered, identified and returned to their families. Because of their tireless work, Veterans of WWII, Korean and other conflicts are now being recovered, and this important work continues.

I have worked on this issue for over twenty-seven years, while stationed at Phu Loi (just north of Saigon), I was alerted to take three Huey Gunships to Khe Sanh (extreme northwest part of South Vietnam) to support MACV's SOG teams during their secret missions into Laos, to gather information on movements of the North Vietnamese Army. The teams usually consisted of three Americans and eight Montagnards, we would insert them into their target area of operation, leave them and come back days later to pick them up. During the two months that I supported this effort, we lost several individuals and one complete team. (We did recover the Vietnamese interpreter a couple days later). I never knew the names of these courageous Americans, because they did not wear name tags. I think of these men often, and a few months ago I asked the National League of Families to try and get the names of these men.

A couple days later, the League sent me their names. They are still missing (MIA to us); their families are still seeking answers and waiting for their recovery.

A few months ago, I was asked to be the National Veterans Adviser for the League of Families. I was honored to be asked and I quickly accepted.

Chapter 14

National League of Families of American Prisoners and Missing in Southeast Asia

MS. Ann Mills Griffiths, the Executive Director, whose brother Lt. Cdr. James Burton Mills, USNR, a pilot flying off the USS *Coral Sea* and was shot down over North Vietnam asked me to be the National Veteran Adviser, she asked me to speak at the annual meeting in Washington D.C. in July 2009. Knowing that I could not possibly make it through the speech, I asked my great friend, the Chairman of the Board of the League, Mrs. Jo Anne Shirley to read it for me. Her brother, Major Bobby Jones an Air Force Flight Surgeon is MIA, they have discovered the crash site, his remains, along with the Pilot should be recovered shortly. This is what I said: I have asked my good friend Jo Anne Shirley to read this for me, I have tried to speak to POW-MIA family groups before and found it an impossible task to me for the reasons I will explain. In 1966, during my first tour in Vietnam as a helicopter pilot, I was asked to take three Huey Gunships from our base near Saigon to Khe Sanh, located in the top Northwest corner of South Vietnam, near Laos and the DMZ.

We were there to support the Green Beret missions, which consisted of 11-man recon patrols. Almost all the missions were in Northeast Laos and were sent in to gain intelligence on the movements of the North Vietnamese Army. The teams usually consisted of three Senior NCOs and eight Montagnards, the indigenous people that lived in the area, they were the bravest of the brave. A few of the team members were wounded, but for the most part, the missions were very successful. Then one fateful day we inserted the team on a hilltop in Laos near the Ho Chi Minh trail, almost immediately, they came under heavy enemy fire, Air Force fighters that were capped and my three Huey gunships attempted to suppress the fire long enough to get the troop helicopters back in for the pick-up, the CH-34's were flown by South Vietnamese pilots who were fearless and were outstanding pilots. I never knew their actual names, they were called Cowboy and Mustascho and were known for their bravery and flying skills. I was told that both were killed in action some time after we left after two months of supporting the mission. Part of that time we were supported by Navy CH-46s, one of which had to sling load my Huey from Khe Sanh back to Da Nang to replace the transmission that froze after landing at the Khe Sanh strip, two minutes earlier and would have crashed in the mountains north of the airfield.

It was impossible to recover the team, day turned into night and we had to leave the battle site. The entire team was lost, we did manage to recover the Vietnamese interpreter a couple days later, he had managed to escape and had a radio, he made contact with us and we picked him up on a hilltop a couple miles from the drop-off point.

All three Americans are still MIAs, I never knew their names as they did not wear name tags. I have never forgotten them, then a couple months ago, I asked Ms Griffiths to see if she could get their names, a couple days later she sent me their names and it was a very emotional time for me and still is. (Note: After the speech a lady approached me, she was very emotional and said her Husband worked those missions also and was still missing in action—I almost lost it again).

So: If this loss affected me this way and still does, one can only imagine how difficult it is for the family members to cope with the loss of their loved ones.

In 1982, I was involved with chartering an L1011 from Delta Airlines and taking 300 Vietnam Veterans and some family members to the dedication of the Vietnam Veterans Memorial in DC. After that I was appointed by President Reagan as the Executive Director of the Georgia Vietnam Veterans Leadership Program and got to know the three Jo Ann's and later Susie, they did a remarkable job of educating the public about the POW-MIA issue.

Later, we started an effort to build a Vietnam Veterans Memorial that would be placed at the State Capitol in Atlanta. We approached the Legislative Committee for funds, got a little push back, we sent them a follow-up letter with this sentence added. "Imagine going home after work today and finding your spouse or child missing, how much time and resources would you expend to find them?" We got the funds, If you visit Atlanta, go to the capitol and visit the memorial, which consists of three bronze life-size figures, a soldier with a radio, calling in a medevac Helicopter, a nurse who is providing medical aid to a wounded soldier. The Memorial was dedicated on Nov. 11th, 1988 and the inscription says:

THIS MEMORIAL IS DEDICATED TO THOSE GEORGIANS WHO FOUGHT, DIED AND ARE STILL MISSING IN ACTION IN SOUTHEAST ASIA. THEY ANSWERED THEIR COUNTRY'S CALL TO DUTY WITH COURAGE AND SACRIFICE AND THEY SHALL NEVER BE FORGOTTEN.

After that we convinced the legislature to pass a law that required the state to fly the POW-MIA flag at all the welcome centers and rest stops.

After I returned to my home state of Arkansas, we began an effort to do the same thing there, Arkansas now proudly flies the flag at their welcome centers.

Several months ago, I sent a letter as the National Veteran Adviser to the League to all the states and territories to inquire if they fly the POW-MIA flag, about a dozen responded that they did, we then began contacting the remaining states and with a little prodding, I can report to you today that all 50 states, Puerto Rico, the Virgin Island, the D.C. mayor's office and the Commonwealth of the Northern Marinas Islands are currently flying the flag. Guam has ordered flags and Liz Flick will send one to American Samoa when she returns home.

In 1993, myself and two friends, Alex Wells Jr. and his wife, Mary Thibaudeau started an effort to make a Vietnam POW documentary, our plan was to take six POWs back to Hanoi and visit the prisons where they were held captive. After months of tireless work and the assistance of several friends, we were able to get permission to film for one month in Hanoi. Time will not allow me to tell you how long and arduous a task that was.

We managed to convince Col Everett Alvarez Jr., the first pilot shot down, Col. Leo Thorsness, Medal of Honor recipient, prior to shoot down, Col. Fred Cherry, the ranking black POW, Col Ben Purcell, the ranking Army POW, Berhardt Diehl, A German nurse and Dat Nguyen, a South Vietnamese pilot. Leo's wife, Gaylee and Ben's daughter, Joy went with us. It was a life changing event for me and you can imagine how it affected the POW's. How they survived is a miracle, but they will tell you, we are the lucky ones, many did not return to their loved ones.

Now, why did I tell you this? Everyone in this room today knows that the League needs to raise funds to continue their outstanding work on behalf of those Americans who are still missing in action and those who may become missing.

If it had not been for the League, the Veteran's Groups and concerned citizens, this issue would have in all probability ceased to exist long ago. We owe these courageous family members more than can ever be repaid for their tireless work on behalf of our comrades.

I have witnessed the magnificent work of these family groups, I have watched the Department of Defense set up procedures, regulations and SOPs that ensured quick and sustained measures to account for those who go missing on the battlefield, they never stop looking.

In the last few weeks, I have talked to countless Veterans and told them about the need for funds to ensure the League could continue their efforts to account for our comrades who are still unaccounted for, to a person, they have said they would help.

I know our Veterans will step up to the plate, we have to come up with a plan to notify them of the situation and they will respond.

Everything I have told you today could not have been accomplished by me—many, many friends gave up their time to make these things happen. We can do this, we just have to pull together.

God Bless the League and their volunteers, God Bless those still unaccounted for, God Bless the family members and God Bless our men and women who are serving our country in the armed forces and God Bless America.

Vietnam vet's plan puts focus on individuals

Documentaries on Tet, POWs in works

By Ron Martz
STAFF WRITER

FRANK NIE

The Tet Vietnam Veterans Reconciliation Project cludes (from left) Vice President Ron Miller, Secretar urer Mary Thibaudeaux and her husband, President / Wells, at their Marietta office.

The defining moment in Alex Wells's Vietnam War experience 25 years ago has become the defining moment in his life.

On Feb. 16, 1968, Mr. Wells, then a young Marine first lieutenant, was surrounded by North Vietnamese troops in the ancient city of Hue during the Tet Offensive.

Certain of his own death, he continued to call in artillery fire ~elieve pressure on the South namese unit he had been as-signed to, when a lucky shot killed the enemy commander, breaking up the attack.

"My life was spared for some reason and I didn't have any earthly reason why for years after," said Mr. Wells, 50, a Roswell resident.

Now, the former St. Simons Island real estate broker believes his life was spared in order to promote reconciliation among former combatants in a war that continues to haunt many of them.

Mr. Wells and his wife, Mary Thibaudeaux, are promoting that reconciliation through the Tet Vietnam Reconciliation Project Inc., which they formed two years ago, and with two television documentaries on which they are executive producers.

The Reconciliation Project will assist war veterans who want to return to Vietnam, an ex- "ence that many have said has ed them deal with the emo-tional and psychological problems that developed because of the war.

The documentaries are the primary focus at the moment, however.

The first, featuring former prisoners of war, was shot in Vietnam in late March by Furman Films of Los Angeles and is expected to be ready for television release in midsummer, according to Mr. Wells.

3 trips since January '92

In June, Mr. Wells and Ms. Thibaudeaux will make their third trip to Vietnam since January 1992 to complete preparations for the second documentary, a retrospective on the Tet Offensive. It will be filmed in September at four locations that were the focal points of the prolonged battle — Hue, Khe Sanh, Marble Mountain near Da Nang and Saigon, now called Ho Chi Minh City.

The POW documentary cost about $400,000, to produce, according to Mr. Wells, with the money coming from the film company, individual veterans and himself. The Tet documentary, which will include interviews with several American and Vietnamese survivors of each of those battles, is expected to cost about $600,000. Funding is still being sought for that film.

"This is not a money-making project for us," Mr. Wells said. "It's more a project of the heart that I feel compelled to do."

Mr. Wells's efforts have won the support of several influential Georgia veterans of the Vietnam War.

Chuck Searcy of Atlanta, executive director of the Georgia Trial Lawyers Association and a Vietnam vet, is one of several veterans assisting Mr. Wells on the Tet documentary.

"We've had great cooperation from the Vietnamese people," Mr. Searcy said, "even though they're puzzled by our reluctance to let go of the war. But it's

almost as if the people are getting ahead of the governments on reconciliation."

Ron Miller, executive director of the Georgia Veterans Leadership Project and a longtime veterans advocate, said the documentaries will be devoid of political messages and will focus on individual soldiers.

'Reconcile the wounds'

"The main reason for doing these documentaries is to help Vietnam vets and their families cope with the problems they've had as a result of the war," said Mr. Miller.

Mr. Wells believes the veter-

an-to-veteran nature of ject helped him and the fi obtain key interviews w Vo Nguyen Giap, the arc North Vietnam's military gy against the French an icans, and Hanoi Han Vietnam War's version c Rose, during the March I

Mr. Wells said he that the Vietnamese gov may be using his efforts promote a normalization tions between the two co

"But," he said, "wh trying to do is recon wounds of war between peoples, not necessarily governments."

Chapter 15

President Bill Clinton

SINCE I was born and raised in Arkansas, graduated from Arkansas State University and moved back to my home state a few years ago, I thought I would say a few words about Mr. Bill. In 1996, I was attending the Republican National Convention in San Diego, California. I had to go to a local post office and mail some material back to the Dole campaign office in D.C. I was standing in line talking to a friend. A couple in front of us noticed my accent and ask me where I was from. I replied Arkansas. They assumed I was a Clinton supporter and asked me if I supported him. I told them no, and that I was the National Chairman, Veterans for Dole. They responded, "We are supporting President Clinton." I responded, "Well, I hope he will not disappoint you, but I think he will."

I met President Clinton three times. My brother, Owen was elected to the Arkansas House of Representatives and served 12 years, all during Clinton's term as Governor. The Veterans of Arkansas lobbied hard for a memorial honoring Vietnam Veterans with success.

My brother, a World War II Veteran was very supportive of Veteran programs in the state and was invited to participate in the dedication ceremonies. My friend General William C. Westmoreland was invited to speak.

My brother invited me and my fiancée, a Georgia Peach to attend the ceremonies and also invited us to a private event in the Governor's office with the Governor at the end of the ceremony. My brother escorted us to a receiving line, where we were introduced to the Governor. He said, "Governor, this is my brother Ron, the Vietnam Veteran that I told you about." I shook his hand and he said, "Let me tell you a story about Owen, he is the only State Representative that I know of, whose car was towed away from the Capitol, because he parked in the Governor's parking spot." We all had a good laugh. Next he was introduced to Mary Ann, he seemed to like her a great deal.

During his last year in office, the local folks decided to give my brother a roast in his home town. Clinton called and told my brother that he was planning to come to the event, which he did. They introduced him. He started his speech with this comment, "I would like to thank Owen Miller for his support in the House of Representatives ... ten percent of the time." Later my brother said the percentage was a little high.

I met Wesley Pruden, the Editor of the Washington Times, at an event in Washington, D.C., and we had a conversation. I told him that I lived in Arkansas and had meet Governor Clinton a couple times. I sent him this letter from Romania:

WHY I WILL NOT BE INVITED TO BILL'S INAUGURATION

First, I am from Arkansas and Bill has had a lot of trouble with his Arkansas friends lately. Many have been indicted, gone to jail, awaiting jail, fired, sent home early and worse.

Secondly, I am sure someone will tell him that 1 was the Executive Director for Veterans for Dole and tried very hard to send him back to Arkansas or Hollywood. Hollywood would be a better choice since he is the best actor to ever become President One only has to remember his incredible ability to change from someone in obvious glee to tragic sadness when caught on film during a Ron Brown memorial event. He pulled out the stops, did you catch the wiping of a non-existent tear worthy of an Academy Award performance.

And I know he knows that the Veteran effort was responsible for alerting the nation's veterans that good old Bill now wanted us to believe that as Commander-In-Chief of our armed forces, he was a VETERAN and protected from civil law suits under the World War II Soldiers and Sailors Relief Act. How's that for acting? The full page ads, in several national newspapers condemning him, for on the one hand, dodging the draft in Vietnam and now using his CIC status to block the Paula Jones sexual harassment lawsuit, caused him and his crack team of lawyers a few sleepless nights. Maybe the media would like to research our nation's history to determine how many Governors have found it necessary to take out two 1 million dollar insurance policies to protect oneself from these types of law suits. Nah! That couldn't happen.

I must tell you that I am writing this editorial from the most unlikely place one could imagine, Bucharest, Romania. A Medal of Honor recipient and a friend of mine, Ron Ray, who has worked in Romania for some time asked me to consider a contract to work on the Romania Presidential run-off elections. I immediately accepted, as I had made plans to attend the Vietnam Veterans Institute's annual Patriot's Day Dinner in D.C. on November 9th I had to leave for Romania on that day, relieved that I would not have to face many of my Veteran friends immediately after our defeat, many of whom I had recruited for the "Veterans For Dole" effort.

I was unable to help defeat Bill Clinton, but the voters of Romania, for the first time in their history changed their government by the ballot box. One out of two in campaign efforts ain't bad.

Anyway, back to Arkansas. I am from West Ridge, a town so small the town limits signs are on one post. At one time, we had a cotton gin, service station and general store. The gin and service station shut down several years ago and some local boys burned down the general store, which had been turned into an auction barn. A mile and a half down the road is Three Way Inn, famous in local folklore because the meanest man in the area put a horse, overnight, in his wife's beauty shop because she filed for divorce. It later burned, but that's another story.

You' all tell Bill to notify his highway patrol buddies in Arkansas that I sold my Lexus with Georgia tags and bought a red pickup truck with my gun in rear window. My coon dog rides in front seat and my girl friend rides in back, a lot easier to get in and out to open up the pasture gates. Now before I hear from all the feminist, let me tell you why I make her ride in the back You see, it all boils down to power. While in Romania I read an article about the gender gap between Bob Dole and Bill Clinton. According to Rosalie Osias, a New York lawyer/writer, working women favored Bill Clinton over Bob Dole 56% to 35% and it has to do with Bill Clinton's projection of personal power than with his lofty, public Ideals. It is an aphrodisiac for them. Well my girlfriend, La Verne works at the I-40 truck stop. I used my power as a former campaign worker and sole owner of my red pickup to make her ride in the back. She's not too sure what aphrodisiac means, but she seems to like It. Hey! It worked for Slick. Why not for me?

Everything in this editorial is true, well not everything. I don't have a coon dog. I could go to Bill's swearing in ceremony, another Medal of Honor recipient invited me to go with him. They sit on the front row. He said I could moon Bill. I said, "Nah! He would probably moon me back and I wouldn't have a follow-up."

President Clinton, from Hope, Arkansas certainly put Arkansas on the map, I was not a supporter, but that's life.

Chapter 16

Home Box Office

ONE of my friends in Atlanta, Georgia, was the Southern Regional Manager for Corporate Affairs and Public Relations for Home Box Office. My first contact with her concerning the movie, "Letters Home from Vietnam," a very emotional movie that shared the stories of the men and women who served in Vietnam, many of them who did not make it home.

I was asked to assist in getting Vietnam Veterans and their families to come to the opening of the movie. We filled the house. I introduced some of the veteran leaders to the audience. We were told that it could cause an emotional reaction among some vets. We were prepared, as we had several mental health care professional on hand. It was very emotional and some did leave the movie from time to time. Some did not come back. Sometime later, I was invited to a private screening of a movie about the trip wire veterans living in the mountains in the state of Washington. John Lithgow starred in the movie (3rd Rock from the Sun star). He did a great job and I had a long conversation with him. He shared his experiences making the movie.

The last time I worked with HBO was to premier the movie "Path to War," starring Donald Sutherland, Alex Baldwin and Michael Gambon. It was directed by John Frankenheimer. Again, we turned out a large crowd of veterans, a couple of POW's and Medal of Honor recipients to preview the movie before it was shown to the public.

The movie was basically an indictment of the McNamara's and the Johnson Administration's handling of the war, which cost Johnson his second term. I have included the HBO letter that I received after the screening.

May 21, 2002

Mr. Ron Miller
Director,
Georgia Vietnam Veterans Leadership Program
69 Brice Road
Dawsonville, GA 30534

Dear Ron:

What a blessing to reconnect with you after all these years! You still have that dynamite charisma and driving dedication to veterans' affairs which comes as no surprise. We regret that the timing of our event was incompatible with the veterans services accreditation school, but we were gratified with the strong presence of Vietnam veterans.

We deeply appreciated your kind and thoughtful remarks before our screening of PATH TO WAR. Like you, we've received many positive responses since the premiere. HBO tells it like it is, and we hope that our collective cinematic reflections on the Vietnam War put the experience in perspective, after all these years, and helps veterans continue their healing process.

I Look forward to hearing about your White House assignment, so please keep me posted. Thanks for everything you do for the vets and the community, Ron. I'm proud to know you! I'm sending best wishes for continuing success in all you do.

Warm regards,

Pat

Pat A. Conner,
Southern Regional Manager
Corporate Affairs and Public Relations

Chapter 17

Jeff Foxworthy

AS I mentioned a couple of times, my quest in life after retiring from the military was to have fun. To that end, I found the perfect home, a ranch style, do not like stairs, that would accommodate a nice cement pond (swimming poll for you sophisticated folks) and hot tub. My old buddy, Phillip Darnell had become a master builder in Atlanta and he set about to make me happy. He did a great job with the pool and he and another good friend, Richard Grant painted huge lobsters on the bottom, small ones that appeared to be going into the small holes in the side of pool and one feature that caused me a little ribbing from my Mom when she visited. At the far wall of the hot tub, they painted sets of the feet, (the bottom of the feet), it was obvious that one set belongs to a man and one to a woman, you guessed it, one was facing up and one facing down. I was giving my Mom a tour of the pool area and when we came to the hot tub, she looked at it and said, "Ron what does that mean?," of course she knew and I remarked, "Oh, my old buddies put that in."

In the summertime, there was always a party at the place. After awhile, there was no need to invite anyone. They just drove by-if cars were lined up, they stopped and came in. I had great neighbors, they never complained about the traffic, well one time someone did call and said the street was partially blocked, the Cop came to the door, asked that all the cars must be parked on one side of the street, I remarked, I hope I can get their attention, he said, if you cannot, I can. The cars were moved quickly.

A girlfriend of mine, who was a flight attendant for Eastern Airlines called one Sunday and asked if she could bring a friend. I said of course, and that she did not have to ask. She replied he is a comedian and could tell some jokes if we wished. I replied, everyone that comes here is a comedian and to come on.

A little later in she walks with Jeff Foxworthy, his Redneck Joke routine had just begun to catch the notice of the public and everyone thought it was hilarious. I took him out to the pool and after a few times trying, finally got everyone to stop talking and Jeff went into his routine. The crowd loved it and asked for more. I don't have to tell you what happened to his career.

Chapter 18

Lee Greenwood

L EE Greenwood had released his incredible song, "God Bless The USA," and was under contract to Coors Beer for some period of time. He was performing to sell-out crowds all over the country, he was very hot. Lucky for us, Coors Beer was possibly the best Corporate Sponsors of Veteran Events in the Country, no one came close. Their best effort was offering scholarships to Veterans and their family members.

I made contact with their national office and spoke to their Director of Public Relations, I explained our program and some of the events we had done with the Atlanta Hawks, Braves, Six Flags over Georgia, etc.

We agreed to assist Coors with a Lee Greenwood concert at Stone Mountain Park, just outside Atlanta. We packed the place with thousands of fans, it was by far the best event we worked in the 13 years I was the ED. We met Lee at a couple of other events, he was always very helpful when it came to assisting Veterans. I took him to meet Zell Miller at the Capitol when he was the Lt. Governor. Zell is a huge Country music fan and is friends with many of the stars. I also introduced him to Governor Joe Frank Harris, a very strong supporter of veterans.

When Newt Gingrich was elected Speaker of the House of Representatives, he invited Lee to attend his party and sing the song. The President of Delta Airlines was there, I asked Lee if he knew him, he said no, but would like to meet him, maybe he could get some endorsement gigs with Delta. I introduced him and they had a very good conversation.

To: Ron
with Best wishes,
Joe Frank Harris

Chapter 19

Arkansas State University Reserve Officer Training Corps Hall Of Heroes

I graduated from Arkansas State University and received a commission to Second Lieutenant through the Reserve Officer Training Corp program. At that time, all males, if physically qualified, had to take ROTC for the first two years If you wanted a commission, you had to sign up for the Advance courses during your Junior and Senior year. I had always considered joining the services, like my father and four brothers.

During my senior year, they announced they had eleven positions for flight training at the local airport. We took tests to determine if we had the aptitude for flight training and I got the last slot. Upon commissioning, I had to serve three years instead of the normal two.

This was one of the best decisions of my life! I thoroughly enjoyed flying and it seemed to come naturally to me, don't know why, but it did. Flying is the reason I spent twenty years in the Army instead of getting out after my normal obligation.

The ROTC Department at ASU established their Hall of Heroes some time ago and it includes some of my friends who excelled in their military service. My name was submitted and it was approved, at which time I was notified that it would be presented by the President of the University and the Professor of Military Science Department at half time at a football game.

They also told me that I could have as many free tickets to the game as I wanted. I informed them that I had a rather large family, no problem, just let them know how many tickets I needed. Fifty-three members of my extended family showed up for the ceremony.

I asked my brother Owen who served during WWII and brother Bob who served in Korea and his Son Matt, a member of The Arkansas State Patrol to join me on the field.

It was quite a ceremony, they presented me with a football painted white with the following information, ASU vs. New Mexico State, October 26, 2002, Game Ball ASU Indians, Presented to Major (Ret)

Ron M. Miller, ROTC Hall of Heroes Inductee. It was quite an honor and I will always remember that evening.

Chapter 20

Vietnam Veterans Memorial Atlanta, Georgia

WE accomplished a lot during the thirteen years that I headed up the Vietnam Veterans Leadership Program in Atlanta, Georgia, thanks to the hard work of countless men and women. I will name some at the end of this book.

One of our accomplishments, that gave me great satisfaction, was the planning, funding and building the Vietnam Veterans Memorial that is located at the Pete Wheeler Memorial Plaza in front of the Floyd Veterans Memorial Building, across the street from the State Capital.

Like a lot of other things we accomplished, it would not have happened had it not been for Commissioner Pete Wheeler, Georgia Department of Veterans Service. A year earlier, he was in Arizona for the unveiling of the state's statue for Vietnam Veterans. He took pictures of the statue and show it to us and said he hoped we would consider a Memorial in Georgia.

Pete told us to meet with Representative Joe Wood, Chairman of the Defense and Veterans Affairs Committee in the Georgia State House of Representatives. He made it happen. The House authorized $ 150,000 for the bronze statue. The plans would call for a seven foot bronze casting of three Vietnam Veterans. One figure is wounded and is kneeling on the ground. He is being treated by a Nurse, while a third with a radio on his back is calling for a MedEvac helicopter. It was the first Vietnam Veterans Memorial that included a female. I wrote the following comments that are etched in the base of the Memorial:

THIS MEMORIAL IS DEDICATED TO THOSE GEORGIANS WHO FOUGHT, DIED AND ARE STILL MISSING IN ACTION IN SOUTHEAST ASIA. THEY ANSWERED THEIR COUNTRY'S CALL TO DUTY WITH COURAGE AND SACRIFICE AND THEY SHALL NEVER BE FORGOTTEN. 11-11-88.

Every time I visit Atlanta, I go by and spend a little time there.

I have heard thousands of speech's in my life time, the best words I heard during most of them were, "and in closing." So how do I finish this, there is only one way, it's to thank the thousands of Veterans, friends, strangers and others for their support, prayers and friendship during the thirteen years that I headed up the Georgia Vietnam Veterans Leadership Program.

The support cut across all spectrum's of society, from the unemployed, the homeless, the corporate world, local, county and state governments, the faculty at colleges and universities, the media, the Veteran Service Organizations and above all the Vietnam Veterans who had waited their turn to be thanked and appreciated for their service.

I fortunately was asked to head up this effort, but the real workers, the ones who made it happened day after day were Tony Hamilton who ran the Employment and Training office, assisted by Mary Thibaudeau and Alex Wells, Jr. for one year toward the end of the program. Andy Farris, who developed an outstanding Small Business Outreach Program, and the Board of Directors: Judge Keagan Federal Jr., Tommy Clack, Mary Lou Keener, Ruby Sellers, Bob Knowles, James Blaylock, Eddie Clermont, Richard Reber, James Mathis, Max Carey Jr., Mike Mantegna, Art Millard, Tom Carter and Del Perkins. All were combat Vietnam Veterans and most were Service Connected Disabled Veterans.

Our volunteers who taught small business seminars, almost always in the evenings were: Andy Farris, Jim Mathis, Richard Schuman, John Medlin, Chuck Reaves, Steve Raines, Dan Wall, Ted Chernake, Max Carey, Jr., John Howe, Howard Segan, Kurt Mueller and Dixon Jones. We also owe a great debt of gratitude to Dr. Mike Mescon, Dr. Tim Mescon and Rodney Alsup at Georgia State University and Kennesaw State College for their support in making this program a success. Also a big thank you is owed to Mr. Henry Pair, the Veteran's Rep at the Atlanta Small Business Administration for his dedication to this program.

The Employment and Training Program placed thousands in full-time career positions and the Small Business Program captured over 60 million dollars in SBA direct and bank guaranteed loans.

Never in my wildest dreams would I have imagined that my life would take the turns that it has. It was not something I thought about or planned. My life was enriched beyond my wildest imagination and I thank God everyday that I took the opportunity to serve others, in my case, Veterans.

At the end of 2008, I received another three year Presidential appointment to the National Advisory Committee, Veterans Business Affairs, U.S. Small Business Administration. I am in my seventh year and will continue as long as I am productive. A special thanks to Bill Elmore, Associate Administrator, Office of Small Business Development, U.S., SBA for getting me involved with the Committee in 2002.

In the end, all this was made possible because of SERVICE TO OTHERS. It reminds me of this quote from Winston Churchill: "We make a living through what we receive for our labors, but we make a life through what we give."

VIETNAM
THIS MEMORIAL IS DEDICATED TO THOSE GEORGIANS
WHO FOUGHT, DIED AND ARE STILL MISSING IN ACTION
IN SOUTHEAST ASIA. THEY ANSWERED THEIR COUNTRY'S
CALL TO DUTY WITH COURAGE AND SACRIFICE AND THEY
SHALL NEVER BE FORGOTTEN.

Chapter 21

A Special Thank You

I would be remiss if I did not pay my respects to Mr. Jan Scruggs, a Vietnam Veteran whose idea it was to build the Vietnam Veterans Memorial. Books have been written about what he and others had to go through to raise the millions, fight back against the naysayers and build the Memorial. Without him the Memorial would have never been built and my life would have been completely different.

I also want to thank Mr. David Adams, Editor of *Aviator*, the magazine for The Vietnam Helicopter Pilots Association for publishing the information about *Dead Men Flying* a book by Major General Patrick Brady, USA (Ret.), with Meghan Brady Smith. General Brady, a Medal of Honor recipient, tells the story of the legend of Dust Off, America's Battlefield Angels. I urge all to read of the incredible bravery of those helicopter pilots who rescued us from the battlefields of Vietnam. I contacted General Brady, who gave me the name of his publisher and encouraged me to contact him. He was also kind enough to endorse my book and I thank him for his consideration.

My sincere thanks to Ray Merriam, owner and publisher of Merriam Press, who agreed to take a look at my book and signed on as the publisher. Google Merriam Press and you can see and read of his dedication to publishing books about our military, especially books written by veterans.

Thanks for taking the time to read about my journey in life, so far. It has been a blast and an experience that I could only dream about as a young boy working in the cotton fields in Northeast Arkansas. I have been asked many times about my service in Vietnam and the three tours flying helicopters in combat. Somehow, I could never seem to adequately express myself about my service to my Country.

Then one day, I came upon this quote from John Stuart Mill that summed up my feelings perfectly: "War is an ugly thing, but not the ugliest of things; the decayed and degraded state of moral and patriotic feeling, which thinks nothing is worth a war, is worse. A man who has nothing which he cares more about than he does about his personal safety is a miserable creature who has no chance at being free, unless made and kept so by the exertions of better men than himself."

Now when someone asks me this question, as they often do, I simply quote Mr. Mill.

About the Author

RON Miller, President of Miller Consulting, began his military career as a Private in the Arkansas National Guard, received a Commission at Arkansas State University and served in the U.S. Army in Germany, Korea, and three combat tours in Vietnam as a helicopter pilot. He was awarded two Distinguished Flying Crosses, two Bronze Stars, 21 Air Medals, two awards from the Vietnamese Government and one from the Korean Government, along with numerous other awards for service.

He is a Master Army Aviator, Paratrooper, and rated in several types of helicopters and multi-engine airplanes. He retired as a Major with over 20 years of service and is a life member of the Veterans of Foreign Wars, American Legion, Disabled American Veterans, Vietnam Helicopter Pilots Association, Military Officers of America Association (MOAA), Khe Sanh Vets, Reserve Officers Association (ROA), Military Order of the World Wars (MOWW), and The Knights Templar.

Mr. Miller was appointed as the Executive Director, Georgia Vietnam Veterans Leadership Program by President Reagan and served in that position for 13 years.

He has received the U.S. Small Business Administration's (SBA) Georgia Veterans Advocate of the Year Award, State Jaycees Service Award, VA Medical Center Service Award, the Georgia Secretary of State Outstanding Citizens Award, The 11-Alive Community Service Award, the National Jefferson Award for Community Service, and President George H.W. Bush's, "Thousand Points of Light Award." President George W. Bush appointed Mr. Miller to the National Advisory Committee, Veterans Business Affairs, U.S. SBA, and is in his ninth year of service.

Ron currently serves as the National Veteran Adviser, National League of Families of American Prisoners and Missing In Southeast Asia.

Mr. Miller worked for U.S. Senators Bob Dole, Mack Mattingly, and Paul Coverdell. He was a Technical Consultant for the movie "Green Berets," starring John Wayne and is an Associate Producer for the POW Documentary, "Beyond Courage: Surviving Vietnam as a POW." He also worked on two local Atlanta TV affiliate POW documentaries. Mr. Miller is currently working as a consultant for the feature movie "Perfume River," set during the TET Offensive of the Vietnam War. He currently resides in Jonesboro, Arkansas.